This Place You Know

Christina Houen returned to study and creative writing when she was fifty-nine, completing an MCA and a PhD. With essays, articles and short memoirs published in journals and anthologies over the last two decades, Christina has built her career as a freelance editor and writer.

Christina Marigold Houen
This Place You Know

Dedication

For ATH

This Place You Know
ISBN 978 1 76041 743 7
© Christina Marigold Houen 2019
Cover image: *Paterson's Curse on the Hay Plains*, pastel painting by the author,
from a photograph by Rob Olver, taken about 2014

First published 2019 by
GINNINDERRA PRESS
PO Box 3461 Port Adelaide 5015
www.ginninderrapress.com.au

Contents

Author's note	7
Prologue	9
Martha's Story	11
A man's town, 1923	13
Settling in	19
Courting	25
A fatal inevitability	35
This place	44
New beginnings	49
Hay days	57
A mother's love	65
Disaster strikes again	69
No exit	73
My war	78
Summer 1946	84
Anna's Story	89
A little world, July 1946	91
Summertime	96
Dad	99
No place for a girl	103
Vera	105
Swede turnips	110
Boys are different	114
Drowning	122
Bad dreams	124
Behind the orange tree	126

Wollongong	128
Schooldays	131
Weekends	135
Beach	137
Return	139
Dad goes	143
Alone	149
Broken down	151
Women's work	154
The drought breaks	159
Accident	161
Fortunes	164
Bobby	170
Neighbours	174
A good education	183
School	188
Homeless	204
Of study and sex	207
Someone steady	213
Return to Arendal, 1996	216
Gympie Hospital, 1988	219
The visit, Sydney Women's Hospital, 1974	223
A visitation, Perth, 1982	226
Goodbye to Arendal, 1996	228
Letter to Martha, 2017	230
The Last Song	**235**
This place you know	237
Epilogue	239
Acknowledgements	241

Author's note

The Hay plains have changed greatly since my childhood. Then, it was open pastureland, with patchy saltbush cover and annual grasses. Now, grains, rice, cotton and vegetables grow under irrigation. The only annual that thrives is Paterson's Curse, with its rough hairy leaves and purple trumpet-shaped flowers, crowding out all other plants in swaths of royal purple and bright green, poisoning horses and cattle if they feed on it for long.

Names of people and some places have been changed to protect privacy. This memoir of my mother's and my experiences is drawn from my memories, archival records, my mother's handwritten memoir, and my imagination. It is my truth as I remember it, and may not correspond to the memories of other living members of my family.

Prologue

If you visit the Hay plains at night when people and the animals they tend are asleep, you will, if you walk far enough, come across a curious sight. An old woman, wrinkled and skinny, sits on a patch of red earth, her head bent, intent on a patient and silent task. Her fingers, knotted and twisted, move nimbly back and forth. It is not wool she is shaping into a simple chained fabric that gleams silvery-grey in the moonlight, but vegetable matter that she unwinds from a large irregular ball lying on the bare earth beside her. Her fingers twist in and out, and the soft, earthy-smelling fabric falls on the red soil, spreading over it, cloaking it with a damp, springy, resilient cover. Soon the bare patch is clothed, and she winds up the ball and pokes it into a string bag she slings over her shoulder. She scrambles up and walks with the help of a knotted stick to another bare patch, and squats, muttering a few sounds in a guttural tongue, laying her stick and bag beside her. She begins again her endless task of restoring a moist, living cover to the plains ravaged by harsh sun and wind and many cloven hooves.

Martha's Story

A man's town, 1923

My first week in Hay is one I swear I'll never forget. It is early February, the first week of the worst month of the year, and the temperature has climbed steadily to reach 114 degrees Fahrenheit. It's evening now, on a Sunday before the start of school term, and the air is still too hot for comfort.

When I arrived a few days ago on the South West Mail, nearly twenty-four hours after leaving Sydney, I left my luggage at the station and walked down the main street. Men stood lounging outside the pubs – of which I counted thirteen – yarning, sipping their beers, keeping an eye on the town's business and the people coming and going. Some of them nodded to me, or raised their hat.

I chose Tattersall's Family Hotel for my first night. It seemed the most socially acceptable one, or at least not as smelly and noisy as some of the others I passed. They sent a man up to the station to fetch my luggage, and I settled into my room upstairs. I lay and rested for a while on the bed, with shades drawn, thankful to be still and alone after the rocking and clattering of the train.

Tatt's is a charming wood-and-brick building, two storeys, with a balcony, white columns and iron lace trimming, and below, a wide shaded entrance area. In its heyday earlier this century, I'm told it was a social hub with its own ballroom, three dining rooms, a billiard room, quarters for permanent residents, and many house staff. But its interiors are shabby now and were almost deserted when I arrived. Apart from a couple of travellers who were breasting the bar, I was the only guest and the only woman, except for the barmaid and the hotelier's wife.

I took an evening walk along the main street that bisects the town.

It's broad and dusty, with many charming nineteenth-century buildings, columned, verandaed, façaded, iron-laced. But I was too travel-weary and homesick to appreciate it. I dined early and alone in the large dining room, picking at mutton chops with brown gravy, potatoes and cabbage, and a dessert of jelly, fruit and custard. The noise in the bar rose as men came in after work, dusty, hot and thirsty, and the six o'clock swill got into full swing. As I passed the bar, I glimpsed men yarning over glasses lined up on the counter, tossing down as many as they could before closing time. Of course it's a ritual in Wollongong too, but here it seems to be the heart of the town, of its energy, its identity.

In my small single room upstairs, it was stifling, and as I lay with only nightie and sheet to cover me, I listened to the hubbub below, the drunken voices rising and falling outside the hotel as some of the men lingered, the thumping in the bar as barrels of beer were changed, a shouted argument on the street, curses and, at last, some sort of quiet.

What have I come to, I thought, as I lay and longed for sleep. The stink of beer and cigarettes and loud, uncouth men's talk, far from my family, hundreds of miles from anywhere I know. What would my parents say if they could see me here in this alien setting? Mother would think it most improper for me to be in these surroundings, and Father would be concerned that I am alone and among men who are so common and coarse.

Morning came at last, and I chose a grey linen skirt and tailored white blouse. As I dressed, I was relieved to see that my sleepless night hadn't marked my face. I breakfasted alone again in the dining room, and looked through the local paper, *The Riverine Grazier*. In a column called 'Doings in Different Districts' was a report of a man at Lockhart who had got into an altercation with three other intoxicated men, and was taken to hospital, where he never rallied. Other news…the sale of a sheep station, the number of divorce petitions in New South Wales in 1922, and the death of one of the heroes who captured the Kelly gang at Ballarat. All in small print beside a huge ad with a grinning harlequin face holding a placard saying 'Wrigleys After Every Meal'.

This is the outback.

Upstairs, I refreshed my lipstick, put on a shady hat, and stepped out into the harsh light. I felt better as I drew near the green, cool shrubbery of the park and saw the handsome red brick and white columns of the new District High School in front of it.

I spent the rest of the morning sitting across from the headmaster at his desk while he discoursed luxuriously about anything that came into his head. He is proud of the new War Memorial High School, and he wanted to impress me, I think, with all the town has to offer. He took me on a grand tour of the school, rattling on about the well-appointed classrooms, the library (yet to be stocked with books), the comfortable staffrooms, one for the men, one for the ladies, with a couch to lie on if one is unwell. He took me out to the entrance and pointed out the bricks made from local clay, the gabled upper storey, the paired white columns marking the entrance. And, of course, the memorial motto on the coat of arms: *Pro Tanto Quid Retribuemus* – For so much, what shall we repay.

When we sat down again in his office, I expected him to talk about the classes I am to teach, the standard of the pupils' learning. But he wanted to educate me about the town. He waxed eloquent about the sacrifices of those who died in the First World War.

'Six hundred and forty-one men enlisted, virtually our entire eligible population. One hundred and thirty-four didn't return. Men whose fathers had built this town from nothing. It was the headquarters for Cobb and Co. coaches, for their Victoria and Riverina runs. Before that, the early squatters ran their sheep and horses on this land, and sent their jackeroos out with rifles to try to stop the surveyors marking out the town boundaries. Of course they failed. Now it's a busy junction of river, road and rail, and centre of the south-western pastoral industry – it's a remarkable place.' He sat back, smiling.

I suspect he had delivered this well-researched speech to each new staff member over the past few days.

I shifted in my chair, wondering what is remarkable about the town, other than the heat and the thirteen pubs that punctuate the broad main street. What sort of a life can I have here, I wondered.

He leaned forward as if to answer my thoughts. 'You'll find life very pleasant here, Miss Tennant. We have the park, the tennis courts, the river. We even have the occasional steamer that still comes through, bringing freight and picking up the wool clip from the stations up as far as Darlington Point. When you take a walk down to the river, you'll see the great iron swing bridge, built to allow steamers to go through. In their heyday, the steamers did the bulk of the wool carting, but now with better roads and the new railway their days are numbered.' He leaned back in his chair and smoothed his silver hair.

With his dark eyes and regular features, he is a handsome man and knows it, and he likes the sound of his own voice. Like me, he told me, he came from the coast, and was shocked at first by the aridity and isolation, the substitution of river for ocean, the great empty sky, and by the people, so provincial, rough and uncultivated. But he has come to appreciate the slow pace of life, the quiet, and the rewards of getting to know an inner circle of people with a more refined set of values – of belonging, in fact, to the upper class of the district.

'This town has much to offer. Some of my young teachers who've come from the coast have liked the way of life here so much they've stayed, settled down, married a pastoralist or a businessman. The social life is good. Country people come from miles around for the social events of the year – the show, the picnic races, the ball. Then there's the Waradgery Club, of which of course I'm a member.' He preened his hair again and lifted his cleft chin so that he was looking at me through lowered lashes down his long, straight nose.

I kept my eyes on his face, but my thoughts went back to the quiet, intellectual life I had led at Sydney University, living in a women's college, studying hard, discussing English and Latin literature and ancient history; then there was the fascinating topic of the eccentricities and misdeeds of the professors, some of whom led scandalous lives, like John Anderson, the libertarian professor of

Philosophy, and Christopher Brennan, drunken poet-professor of English literature. I loved it, and I loved my holidays at home when I could talk to Father about the finer points of Roman civilisation, and chat with Mother about local gossip, college life, my women friends, and the occasional scandals.

The head cleared his throat, calling my mind back to his introduction to everything that he considered I need to know as a young single woman coming to an established rural community with a social hierarchy. 'But you have to be invited to join the club – we have top public servants like the district surveyor, the magistrate, and of course the doctors and pastoralists and station managers. It's important from the beginning,' he said with a complacent smile, 'to mix with the right set of people. Especially for a young, well-educated, single woman like yourself. There are some strong women's groups here – the CWA, the hospital auxiliary, the Red Cross, and of course, the church groups. Hay is not exactly a man's town, you know.'

But it is exactly, I thought, remembering the loungers leaning against the posts outside the multiple hotels and the drinkers hanging over the bar, cursing, arguing, storytelling, cackling over lewd jokes.

'Those goats,' he said, looking out the window at a small flock, which was eating the overhanging foliage of the shrubs in the garden opposite, 'are not…well, not exactly characteristic of Hay, you know.'

But they are exactly, as I discovered on my long evening walks over the next few days. The town is laid out with an extensive common on its eastern fringe, and residents have the right to graze their stock there – cows, hobbled horses and above all goats, which belong to the drovers and rural workers who live near the common and share its often scanty vegetative cover. And every day, the goats invade the residential streets in search of what they can devour of people's gardens.

The head arranged for me to board with a couple who live fairly near the school, so I didn't have to sleep a second night at Tatt's. They are childless. He is a bookkeeper at Maclure's Drapery, a kindly, intelligent man. His wife must have been a very pretty woman, but now she is puffy and wears too much make-up, and sometimes douses herself in lily of the valley perfume. When I come home from school, she is waiting for me, and quizzes me about my day, which children were troublesome, and gossips about their families, and advises me how to deal with the children.

One afternoon she stayed in her room with a headache and didn't come out for the evening meal, so I heated some leftovers for tea and sat making awkward conversation with her husband. Little did I know the secret she was hiding from me.

Settling in

34 Pine Street, Hay NSW
2 May, 1923

Dear Mother and Father,
    I hope you are both well and in good spirits.
    You'll see from the address that I've moved. My last landlady was rather erratic, not to say volatile. In fact, I found out after they left town that she is an alcoholic. I'm surprised I didn't realise, but I've no experience of such a type, and she was very cunning at concealing her drinking. Her poor husband did his best, but she even had a mild attack of DTs at one time; she wouldn't let me near her, but relied on the services of a neighbour, who afterwards told me the truth. She went away soon after her descent into DTs and didn't come back; she left me to pack her things for her, and they started a shop in Echuca, where they had lived previously. I think, looking back with hindsight on what she told me of her mother, that her alcoholism, or the tendency to it, was inherited. She was difficult to live with, because she simply could not abstain from trying to run one's life, from interfering in all one did, and it was hard to fend her off, because she was wholeheartedly helpful and generous. It was a great relief to me when she left.
    I'm happy in the new lodgings. The house is on the same street as the school. The owner is an elderly widow of Irish descent. Her husband had been a station-hand on a property in the Booligal district, and she had a life of hardship, which she seems to have endured with fortitude and self-respect. She is always decently dressed and keeps up her cherished standards. One of her sons, an unmarried man in his thirties, lives with her. His choice of jobs is limited, she tells me, by his lack of formal education; what little her children learned was imparted to them from time to time by the bookkeeper on a neighbouring station, out of the kindness of

his heart. Her son drives a baker's delivery cart, and I see him sometimes pull up outside the gate and drop over into the garden to kneel down and study his delivery list. I'd like to help him improve his reading, but fear I would be intruding, and he would be embarrassed and ashamed. The landlady's sister is a frequent visitor to the house. In the country, they lived within walking distance of one another, and when one was expecting a baby, the other would push her youngest child in its pram to the boundary fence, get herself and the pram through as best she could, and take charge while her family at home looked after itself. They are two kindly, sensible women, a welcome change after my former landlady.

Autumn has come at last, bringing softer weather and a few showers. It is such a relief, after three months of hot, dry, dusty days, and late summer storms. I enjoy walking through the park to the river. The park is an oasis. It is spacious and shady, with big trees and green lawns and beds full of luxuriant rose bushes, which seem to love this extreme climate and the abundant horse manure the gardener spreads around them. The school takes up one corner of the park and is approached by well-kept, shady paths.

The Murrumbidgee is like no river I've seen before. It is a magnificent body of water, they say, in good seasons, wide and green. It's been a long, very hot summer, and the winter rains haven't started yet, so it is narrower and shallower now, but still charming, curving its way through the low-lying river flats, shaded by families of red gums – massive old-man ones, slender middle-aged ones, and saplings.

Mother, is your cough gone? One of the teachers at school swears by Hearne's Bronchitis Cure. Personally, I think steam inhalations with eucalyptus, like you used to make us have, are the best.

Father, now that you have retired from the *South Coast Times*, I imagine you have time to read to your heart's content and keep the garden beautiful. They will miss you, though, at the paper, after so many years of your quiet, professional leadership. I think of your high standards when I read the local paper here, which mixes local gossip and important national news with sheep prices, reports of drunken assaults, divorce statistics, notices, and, in a central place, advertisements for floor polish, soaps, chewing gum, bronchitis cures, and other household trivia.

I am well, and at the weekends, I've started making some winter dresses. My landlady lets me use her Singer; a good old treadle like yours, Mother. I'll tell you about the dresses in the next letter.

I have some marking to do before my classes tomorrow, so I'll say goodbye for now.

With much love,
Your affectionate daughter,
Martha

*

When the winter rains come, the river swells, creeping over the shallow banks to cover the grassy floodplains and immerse the gums, which thrive on this baptism. The birds multiply overnight. Ibis, egrets and waders congregate in communities of plenty. I've fallen in love with the grey teal ducks, dabbling and upending in the shallows for riverweed. I wonder why they are called grey when they are far more colourful than that. Their creamy feathers are patterned like scalloped flower petals radiating out from the neck and up from the belly, edges shading from bark-brown to glossy dark chocolate. They mate and make their nests lined with down in rabbit burrows or tree hollows and in spring will hatch out clutches of fluffy brown bundles.

I'm working hard to bring my students up to the standard I expect of them. They are very behind. In the senior classes, I teach English and Latin – the latter only to the academic students. With my Leaving Certificate Latin class, when we've done the grammar drill, we're reading Caesar's *Gallic Wars*, which is rather dry stuff, and Virgil's *Aeneid*. I get them to translate it, a laborious process, and then I read them John Dryden's marvellous translation: 'Arms and the man I sing…'

At night, when my preparation and marking is done, I read Cicero in the Loeb edition, with the Latin text on one page and the translation on the other. Cicero came to politics through the law, and his skill in oratory won him a seat in the Senate. I admire him because he was loyal to the idea of Roman Republic despite his exile by the triumvirate of Caesar and co. A successful legal practice was a very good training for a career in politics, to which most upper-class Romans aspired. It was an absorbing and satisfying career.

I would have loved to study law, but Father said it was not a suitable profession for a lady. Indeed, although the first female law student graduated from Sydney University in 1902, it wasn't until 1918 that women were entitled to practise in New South Wales. I was already training to be a teacher by then. Perhaps if I have daughters, the profession may be more open to them. I knew that I'd be bonded to teach in country schools, as the Education Department has trouble getting unbonded teachers to go there. So far I've been to Dubbo and Grafton, but Hay is rather a shock – the most inland town I've been to.

Certainly, if I have sons, I hope at least one of them will take up the law. Thomas Cromwell is a great example of a man who rose from humble beginnings, trained in law, and became a trusted servant and adviser to Henry VIII. He was blessed with a logical mind in an age sadly devoid of logic, and his legal training put him a cut above most of the other courtiers with aristocratic backgrounds.

We have no aristocracy to speak of in Australia, apart from the few remaining landowners with roots in the English aristocracy. It is so evident that here, as an Englishman once remarked, the top dog's under, and has been for most of the time. Hoi polloi rule, and I fear the study of Greek and Latin, once considered the ticket to a good education, is in its dying days. Certainly, my students have to be pushed to apply themselves. I don't expect my children, if I have any, will share my passion for the Classics.

I've made friends with one of the older women who teaches history and I talk mostly to her at lunchtimes and recess. We share our pleasure in ancient history, and my knowledge of the Roman civilisation fits well with her readings of ancient historians like Herodotus and

Thucydides. I'm friendly with the others, but I avoid their gossip about the men they are interested in and the latest fashions.

When spring comes, I feel restless. To keep my mind occupied when I'm not preparing lessons or marking work, I'm making a couple of new dresses – one of forget-me-not-blue silk, draped softly in the bodice, and a simpler one in apricot and white striped seersucker, with a V-neck and a softly ruffled collar, for casual wear. I got my landlady to mark the hems for me at calf length, and I've nearly finished hemming them. I can't abide the vulgar new fashion for knee-length skirts. Myrtle, a young blonde woman who teaches in the primary school, wears the new flapper-style dresses that hang loosely over her boyish figure; she probably wears one of those new girdles that squash the breasts into a most unfeminine flatness. She smokes too and has a loud laugh. I've watched her playing tennis with her escort. He deserves someone less common, more ladylike. He's slim and lithe, with a shock of thick black hair brushed back from his forehead. His eyes are the same colour as the silk dress hanging in my wardrobe.

I wonder when I will have a chance to wear it. He has a strong hearty laugh and walks with a fluid swing of his hips, shoulders back, head held high.

Today I was in the draper's shop buying some lace to trim a petticoat to wear in the holidays when I heard his laugh, but didn't look round. He was in the men's section and must have seen me, because next thing I knew, he touched my arm.

'Hello. I'm Henry Anderson. I've seen you when I've been playing tennis. My friends tell me you're the new senior Latin and English teacher.'

We exchanged pleasantries, and I accepted his offer to walk me back to my lodgings. We stood outside the gate making small chat, and he took my hand and asked me to walk with him down to the river tomorrow evening when he finishes work. I was a bit taken aback, and pulled my hand away.

'Oh…I thought that you and Myrtle are stepping out together?'

A flush spread over his ruddy skin. 'Oh…we have been, but she's going soon. She's being shifted to another school in the mid-west… I think she has family out there and wants to be near them.' He pulled a leaf off the crepe myrtle that hung over the fence, and crumpled it up. 'This will be in flower when you return after Christmas. It's a beautiful flower…thick plumes of it, crinkly and wrinkly like crepe paper. They come in white, pink, red and deep mauve. I wonder what colour this one is.'

'Oh, yes, they were in flower when I first came – soft pink. They do grow on the coast, but they seem to love this climate. I've never seen such abundant flowers on them as here.'

'So…will you walk with me tomorrow evening?'

'Yes, I should like that.'

'I'll come round at five-thirty. Good night.'

'Good night, Henry.'

He lifted his hat and gave me one of his crinkly-eyed smiles, and swung off down the street.

I'll wear the seersucker…just need to sew the lace around the hem of the petticoat. I am just a little excited, I must admit. I like his energy and his easy, open manner. I wonder if his family are among the Waradgery set the head lectured me about.

Courting

We walk every evening now, and sit for a while on a bench under the trees, watching the river slide past.

He tells me of his dream of a place of his own on the river. 'Since I was a little tyke, sitting with Father on his horse as he rode around checking the fences, out on The Cubas, I've known this is what I want. A little place will do; just enough to run a flock of merinos, breed them for fine wool, and sell off the wethers for meat. It'll have to be on the river, though. The Hay plains are fierce, rain is scarce, and you need access to the river.'

'Tell me about your father's place.'

'Well, Dad was a jackeroo on Illillawa when he first came out to Australia from England. Illillawa was huge in those days, half the district. It's up for sale now. It still has a twenty-three-mile frontage to the Murrumbidgee, and stretches way north of the railway line, up around the Lachlan. The Cubas is a small leasehold that was divided off when they brought the Land Settlement Act in, so more small squatters could have a go. Illillawa is still about 123,000 acres. It used to cover a hundred and fifty square miles, and there were a hundred people working there.'

'Yes, I saw a notice in your agent's window about the sale. How long was your father working there?'

'About nine years, I reckon. He was only sixteen when he came out from England. So he would've been about my age when he took up the lease on The Cubas.'

'If you don't mind me asking – how old are you?'

'Twenty-five. Still a bit wet behind the ears,' he said with a boyish grin.

Three years younger than me! He hasn't asked me my age.

'Does he still run it?'

'Nah, he sold up a couple of years ago; Mother had moved into town with us kids a few years before, so we could finish our education. But Dad kept the lease on and used to ride into town on his motorbike at the weekends, fifty miles on a potholed corrugated road through black soil plains in all weathers. He's a tough old bloke and kept on even though he had arthritis all through his body. But Mother talked him into giving up the lease in the end.'

We sit in silence, watching a family of grey teal ducks foraging in the long grass on the bank. Henry picks up a gumnut and shies it at them, and they stretch their scalloped wings and land on the water at a safe distance near the opposite bank. The ripples spread out around them, and all is peaceful once more.

Henry's forget-me-not eyes are far away.

'What was your life on The Cubas like?'

He turns and smiles, his eyes meeting mine. 'Oh, it was grand. The house had a big central arcade and when we were little we played there. The gauze door into the living room was broken. We weren't allowed in there but I was small enough to crawl through the hole, and sometimes I'd climb into the hollow middle part of Dad's roll-top desk and go to sleep.'

'Oh, it sounds lovely.'

The shadows are getting long and the sky is catching fire.

I look at my watch. 'Well, I'd better get home. I've still got some marking to do for the end-of-year Latin exam papers.'

Henry rests his hand on my elbow as we walk up the uneven path to the park, and leaves it there until we reach my gate. He squeezes my hand and opens the gate for me with his other hand. 'Shall we walk again tomorrow?'

'Yes, I'd like that. I'll be going home for the summer holidays next week.'

'Would you like to come and meet my parents before you go?'

'Thank you, I would.'

I find it hard to concentrate on marking. My thoughts are of a little boy squeezing himself through a hole in the gauze and curling up under his father's desk. And of forget-me-not eyes.

*

Myrtle's friends on the primary staff look at me askance, and I'm sure they're gossiping about Henry's treachery so soon after Myrtle. I'm not concerned, as they are not my friends or equals. I think he thought Myrtle was fun, but I'm sure now he wasn't serious about her.

They live in a house not far from the school called Beaumont. Henry gives me a little history of their family on the way to the house. He has two brothers living, one studying medicine, one doing law. The eldest started a career in banking but died of the pneumonic plague in 1919. So now the household consists of the mother, father, Florence, the youngest child and only daughter, and Henry.

'Flo's a year younger than me. She wants to be a nurse, but Mother and Father won't allow it until she's older.'

'Oh, that's a shame. I think nursing is a very worthy profession, one of the few that women can have a career in. Teaching is too, of course; but since I wasn't allowed to study law, I wanted to be a journalist, like Father. But he said it's an even less suitable profession for a woman than law is, so I did an arts degree and went into teaching.'

'And a very good teacher you are, I hear. Here's Beaumont.'

We step through the white wooden gateway, framed by a trellis with a climbing rose in full flower, small single pink flowers with white eyes.

'What a lovely rose!' I reach up to touch a blossom.

'It's a Ballerina. Father and I are very proud of our roses. We feed them with horse manure from the race course.'

Henry's mother rises to meet me as we walk into the lounge room. She is tall and slim and elegantly gowned, with curly hair still dark brown, just a few threads of grey, and big brown eyes. She holds out her hand with a warm smile and gestures to me to sit down in the comfortable armchair opposite her. Her husband comes in as I sit, and walks over a little haltingly, slightly bent. He greets me and shakes my hand; his fingers are knobbly, his palm calloused, and his grip is strong. He sits in an upright chair nearby, grunting slightly as he eases himself down.

Henry throws himself onto the chaise longue by the window, one arm across the curved back, one resting loosely on his thigh. His eyes are on his mother's face.

'I'm sorry Florence isn't here to meet you, Miss Tennant. She's visiting her cousins in Adelaide. Now, how do you like your tea?' She gestures to Henry, who jumps up and pushes the trolley over to her side.

As I sip the good strong Ceylon tea and nibble a Melting Moment, Mrs Anderson tells me stories of life in the country and her childhood on her father's stud station near Booligal.

'Well, you know, we kept our standards up, though it was hard work. We had a maid who did a lot of the rough work but we all had jobs to do. We cooked, swept the floors, helped with the washing, mending, and ironing. We didn't have any formal schooling; we had a succession of tutors and governesses.'

'What were they like?' I asked. I had thought of applying for such a job myself when I first started my training, as I had a romantic idea of life on the land, and a secret dream of marrying a landowner. But I was afraid of being trapped in an unsavoury household like Sybylla in *My Brilliant Career*, when her father fell on hard times and she took a job as a governess.

'Well, most of the governesses were spinsters obliged to earn the best living they could in a socially acceptable fashion, and very much concerned with correct behaviour and with social standards in general. There were some tutors. They were mostly remittance men sent out by their English families, either because they had been in some sort of trouble and were a source of embarrassment, or because of poor health. The expectation was that they would stay away. Unfortunately, several of the ones we had were unreliable. They would go into town on their days off and get drunk, and some just didn't come back. It was always a struggle to keep the children's education going. That's why we moved into town, so the boys could matriculate and go on to university or professional careers.'

'What about Florence?' I ask, wondering how it would be to be the youngest and female, with older brothers who were expected to leave home and make their careers. I am the eldest in my family.

Mrs Anderson exchanges glances with her husband, who grunts and shifts in his chair. 'Well, she hasn't done high school. She has a Qualifying Certificate. She wants to be a nurse, but we don't think she's ready to live away from home yet.'

I can tell that is a closed door. I feel sorry for Florence, and hope she will manage to persuade them to let her go. It was never an issue in our house. Father and Mother expected Irene and me to matriculate and go on to university if we wanted to. Perhaps it is different out here in the outback; perhaps women are still living nineteenth-century lives. I realise how fortunate I am to have an enlightened father who believes that women have professional roles to play too, even if law and journalism are still out of reach.

Henry does a round with the teapot for second cuppas like me and his father. And offers me a slice of sponge cake from the trolley. I smile across at Mr Anderson, who seems content to sit and listen to his wife reminisce. He clearly adores her and I can see why. As does Henry.

'Did you have much social life when you were young?' I ask, putting my empty cup on the small oak coffee table beside my chair, and taking another bite of the feather-light sponge.

'Oh yes! Neighbours from far and near came in carriages and on horseback to enjoy my parents' hospitality. We had a stock of spare mattresses stuffed with poultry feathers and stored between the ceilings and roofs of the bedrooms. When we had a big crowd to stay, they were taken down and laid side by side on the floors of the guest rooms. Sometimes we had to rush around and make up beds and do extra baking and get the boys to kill some poultry, for Father would come home from town and announce that he'd asked So-and-So and Such-and-Such out for the weekend. We had picnics and tennis in the daytime and dancing on the wide verandas and in the arcade at night. Mother would play the piano and Father would accompany her on his mouth organ.'

She sighs and leans back. 'Our life here is very quiet in comparison. I was very active in the Red Cross and the Church, but I simply haven't the energy now, and dear George's arthritis slows him down,' she says, looking across at her husband with fond eyes.

I get the impression that her husband doesn't mind a quiet life; he seems more reserved, more English, than his wife and his youngest son. His manner is friendly, but he's hardly said more than a sentence since I arrived. I wonder if Mrs Anderson misses those lively days of her youth; but I imagine that bringing up five little ones without much help would have used up all her energy. And from what Henry tells me, Mr Anderson was a small leaseholder compared to her father, who had a name as a stud breeder and a large acreage. So she wouldn't have had the same household help that her mother had. And the boys wouldn't have done much inside work.

She looks at me and smiles. 'But we have the Waradgery Club, the picnic races, the annual agricultural show, and other events when pastoralists and station managers and their families come to town and join in festivities. And there's the tennis club. Do you play tennis?'

'Oh, not really. I've never been any good at sport. I like to watch tennis and cricket, but I'm afraid I'm no good with a racket or a bat.' I glance across at Henry, who is grinning. 'But I've watched Henry play. He's very good.'

'Yes, he is. But we're glad that he plays less tennis now, and has more time for helping George in the garden.'

'Oh, Mother, you just didn't approve of my tennis partner. She's left town now anyhow.' Henry crinkles his eyes at me, and I drop my gaze.

I feel uncomfortable with the implication that he is now my suitor. I've had a few men pay me attention, at university and in my last posting, but none of them has appealed to me. He is, I confess, the first man who has stirred me. Everything about him, his energy, his lively nature, his hearty laugh and mischievous sense of humour, the way he swings his hips when he walks, his looks, his tender blue eyes... He is comfortable in his skin, relaxed and full of energy, and when I'm with him, I don't feel shy; I feel as though I can just be myself.

His father and mother exchange glances, and there is a palpable silence.

Mrs Anderson smiles warmly at me as if to let me know that they approve of me. 'Now, Henry, perhaps you'd like to show Martha round the garden? I'm going to rest for a little while.'

Her husband levers himself off the chair and comes over to help her up.

She holds my hand and says, 'I'm so glad you've come to live in Hay. I look forward to getting to know you better.'

Mr Anderson walks with us to the garden. 'Don't let Henry brag too much. He thinks he's the gardener. I've taught him everything he knows about growing roses and fruit trees! Goodbye, Miss Tennant. We hope you can visit again before you go home for the holidays.' He turns and limps off to the shed.

While Henry walks me round the garden naming the flowers and shrubs, I am quiet, wondering if I could live a life such as his mother has, working so hard physically, bearing children, if my health would be robust enough, and how it would be to live so far from my family and the coast. I don't imagine life in the outback is anything but hard unless one has the means to hold big acreage and employ domestic help and stockmen.

But when Henry walks me home and talks again of his dream of a place on the river, I feel strangely happy and hopeful. We've been keeping company for about three months now, and though he hasn't asked me to marry him, I know the question is in the back of his mind. I'm still a little unsure, so I'm glad the long holidays are coming up soon, and I'll have time to think it over at home and talk to Mother and Father about it.

*

I visit them again before the end of third term. Mrs Anderson greets me and serves tea but then excuses herself, saying she needs to rest for a while. Mr Anderson sees her to the door, then sits in a chair near me with a second cup of tea. I ask him about his time on The Cubas, and he talks of all the improvements he made to it.

'Well, I had a leasehold called western land lease; it has a limited term and at the end of that term the land has to be surrendered and relet. The holder's compensated by the Crown for the improvements, you know, but the compensation is meagre, and they base it on the condition of the fences and buildings at the time rather than on their cost. Most holders, you know, with an eye to the main chance, they just exploit the land and let the improvements run down. You can sell the lease at a price of eighteen pence per acre for each year the lease has to run but most reckon it's not worth putting money back into development and maintenance. I didn't see it that way. I looked after the place as if it were mine for keeps, and I built homestead, yards, sheds, stockyards, fences, everything it needed to run the place well.'

'Did you sell the lease when you left?'

'I did but I only got five thousand pounds for the leasehold and the improvements. Some say I was a fool for my pains, but I reckon we should put our best into whatever we do.' He sighs and leans back. His face is creased with pain.

I feel sad for him, but do not know what to say, so I change the subject. 'Is your wife unwell, Mr Anderson?'

'Her heart isn't as strong as it used to be. Sometimes she needs to take a tablet and rest for a while. And…our eldest son's death affected her badly.'

'Yes, I'm so sorry. Henry told me he died of pneumonic flu. Such a tragedy for one so young.'

'He didn't matriculate because of his broken education on the property so he went into training as a bank officer living in the bank in Newcastle. They found him on a Monday morning. He'd died sometime during the weekend.'

'Oh, how dreadful! I read reports of the flu epidemic. Apparently, it killed more people worldwide than the Great War, mostly young healthy people in their prime. And it was very sudden. You could be healthy when you woke up and dead by evening.'

'Yes.' Mr Anderson pauses and clears his throat. 'When he didn't turn up at his desk one Monday morning, they checked his quarters and found him dead. We received a telegram the next day. Poor Fanny's never got over the shock of it.'

*

When I come back from the Christmas holidays, Henry and I resume our walks, but a little later in the evening, as February afternoons are fierce until the sun drops behind the bend of trees along the river. I thought about him a great deal while I was at home, and talked about him to Mother and Father. I showed them a photo of him wearing his tennis whites, and they exclaimed how handsome he is. I hinted that I expect a proposal from him, as I wanted to know how they would feel about me marrying him and living in the outback. Father said that I must do what my heart and my reason guide me to do. He knew that once I became a teacher, I would be living away from home a lot, and he wants me to have a life of my own. Mother was a little more uncertain, as she has never travelled or lived independently, and she is afraid of great distances. But when I told her about his family, their pastoral background, his mother's good breeding, his father's

Norwegian lineage, and about the beautiful Murrumbidgee River, the wide open skies and clean air, she seemed a little reassured. I found myself arguing for a life on the land, even though I am still not sure. I do enjoy his company and feel deeply drawn to him, but I must be careful. It's a very serious commitment to make.

As we sit on the bench by the river, watching the slow-moving water, he tells me how much he's missed me, how dull his life has been while I was away. And he asks me if I would like to live with him on a place by the river.

'We wouldn't have much at first you know. Father says he will help me to stock a place if I can get a suitable lease, but he's converting Beaumont into flats to provide an income in their old age, and I don't think he has much to spare.'

'Oh, Henry, let's wait and see. I've only known you for a few months. I'm not sure if I'm suited to be a grazier's wife… I've always wanted a life surrounded by books and ideas, like my father, and I'm not sure if I'm robust enough to live in the outback…the climate, you know, the isolation…and I'd be so far from my family.'

'Martha, I know it would be a big change for you, but I would love you to be my wife. I've never met anyone like you.' He leans closer and puts his arm around me.

I hesitate, then let him kiss me for the first time. For a few moments, I forget where we are. My heart is racing, my cheeks feel hot, and my stomach is fluttering. His mouth is hot and tender, and I feel my reserves melting away…

A sudden loud crack and a splash startle me and I pull back. A branch has fallen from an overhanging tree into the river.

'Henry, let me think about it,' I say, moving away a little on the seat, and tucking a lock of hair back behind my ear. 'I'm not sure, I need time. It would mean a big change in my life. I do like you very much, but I'm not sure if I am meant to be a farmer's wife.'

'All right, Martha,' he says, laughing and jumping up. 'I can wait. I'll ask you again. I don't give up easily. Come on, I'll walk you home.'

A fatal inevitability

34 Pine Street
Hay, NSW
15 February, 1924

Dear Mother and Father,
   Well, the school year has started again, and I have a new senior class in Latin, and a new junior one in English, so I am very busy.
   I hope you are both well. Thank you for the summer holidays. It was lovely to spend time with you both and to breathe the fresh coastal air and feel the sea breezes again.
   Father, I hope you haven't had any more bad turns; have the new pills your doctor prescribed helped? And I hope you've been able to resume your teaching at the Sunday School; I'm sure they have missed you.
   And Mother, is your cough better? Summer colds can be harder to shake off than winter ones. I hope you've been able to sing in the choir again.
   I wonder how Irene is getting on with her new posting at Wollongong Primary? I imagine she's glad to be at home, even though she might prefer to teach Secondary French, which she was trained for. But the posting in Sydney was hard for her, such big classes and unruly children. Please tell her I'll write at the weekend.
   This letter will be short I'm afraid, as I have to prepare my classes for tomorrow. I just wanted to let you know I am well despite the inevitable heat, and my lodgings are as comfortable as ever.
   I see Henry most days; we walk in the evening when it's a little cooler. His mother is very frail; she has to rest a lot, and her husband seems quite depressed. I think he is afraid of losing her. He is so devoted. Henry is well, in robust health in fact, and thinks

he may have found a suitable place on the river. He's told me about it but I haven't been to see it yet.

As I told you when we talked about him, I've known since the end of last year that he is serious about me and that he wants to have his own place. Last week, after I returned here, he asked me to marry him, but I am unsure if I can commit to a life on the land so far from you and from civilisation. I miss our conversations and your wonderful library of books, Father. And I miss our chats over a cup of tea, Mother. I wonder how you both feel about this prospect. It is a big step to take and I've told Henry I need time to think about it and to discuss it with you.

I must say goodbye for now, and get on with my work.

My dearest love to you both, and love to Irene.

Your affectionate daughter,

Martha

*

I'm woken at dawn by a soft knocking on the window. I jump out of bed, wrap my dressing gown around me and part the heavy velvet curtains. In the half-light, I see Henry's face. His eyes are swollen and his usually ruddy face is pale and creased with grief. I push the window up a few inches.

'Henry! What's wrong, and why on earth are you here at this hour?'

'Martha! It's Mother! She died during the night. A heart attack. The doctor's been and written the death certificate.' He puts his hand on the sill and I cover it with mine.

'Oh, Henry, I'm so sorry. Was it sudden?'

He chokes back a sob and takes out his handkerchief to blow his nose. 'Yes. She seemed a bit more tired than usual last night and went to bed early. But there was no warning, no warning.' He pulls his hand away and covers his face, and when he can speak again, he doesn't meet my eyes but lifts his head and straightens his shoulders. 'I'd better go. Father and Flo need me. Come and visit soon.'

Dead at fifty-six, far too young.

Mr Anderson is heartbroken, and his sorrow is compounded by the Anglican minister's refusal to bury her in the Anglican section of the cemetery because she was baptised a Presbyterian, even though she's been a regular churchgoer and active helper. She's buried in the non-denominational section of the cemetery with an imposing gravestone. Under the usual description of her as 'Beloved Wife' of George and the date of her death are the words 'Love's Last Token'.

I recognise the words from a poem of Wordsworth's. It is an apology for the poet's inability to sing of flowers sketched by a lady who is an English emigrant living (and dying) in Majorca. The poet gracefully turns this into an imaginative comparison of the flowers with English ones. He imagines her choosing the sweetest flower and asking for it to be sent to her native land as 'true love's last token'. Mr Anderson must have known this poem and chose the closing phrase as her epitaph because it fitted his image of her as an elegant cultivated flower that bloomed and died in an environment unlike that of her British parents, and his desire to create a lasting memorial to their love.

*

34 Pine Street
Hay, NSW
4 April, 1924

Dear Mother and Father

I hope you are both well, and life is going on at the usual serene pace.

I have exciting news. Henry has taken a leasehold on the river, about twenty-four miles east of Hay on the north side, which is better land, he says, than that on the south side. I went to see it with him at the weekend.

I wish you could see it. The landscape is so different from the coast. The plains are flat and stretch out in a huge arc to meet the horizon. The only thing breaking the circle is the belt of trees that winds along the river's course, called the bend. At this time of year, before the winter rains have come, the plains are very bare, with big expanses of red soil, and patches of dun-coloured dry grasses.

An occasional windmill or a group of stunted trees, and the wavering line of fence posts break the monotony. But once you turn in off the road and approach the river, it changes. The soil darkens to a softer brown, the dry grass and weeds are longer and thicker, and the trees, which look almost browny-black from a distance, reveal a subtler palette of grey-green and darker green, with dark, twisted trunks and branches.

Homestead is too grand a name for the little cottage and rudimentary outhouses. The house itself is only two bedrooms, with wide verandas front and back. At least they are gauzed in. The bathroom, believe it or not, is a shed on the riverbank, open-fronted to the river. And the toilet is a little outhouse with a seat over a pan; when the pan is full, Henry tells me, it is emptied in a hole in the ground. Primitive, I know, but when water is scarce, it is the most hygienic way of disposal. And I suppose the soil benefits.

But there is a decent fuel stove in the kitchen, and wide windows facing the north. And quite a long living room. The kitchen looks out on a citrus orchard, and there are the makings of a garden around the house, with privet hedges planted. On the north side of the garden, there is a row of twelve stately white gums, which give the home an inviting aspect.

I was, I admit, a bit shocked when I first saw it, especially the bathing shed and the toilet (which doesn't deserve that name, so henceforth I'll call it the lavatory), but as we walked around, and Henry told me of his vision for the garden and orchard, and his plans for improvements to the house and sheds, I began to catch some of his fire and to feel we could be happy here and raise a family. The banks of the river are steep near the house, and on the south side, there is a deep bend of trees enclosing the river on both sides. We walked down through the bend and found a couple of lovely sandy beaches.

'Our children can swim safely here,' he said.

Yes, I know that was a presumption on his part!

'The river is the saving grace of this country; it would be impossible to live a decent life out on the plains. But the river will give us water all year round, enough to irrigate the home paddocks, and plenty of fish and wildfowl for eating, and best of all, coolness and shade on hot days.'

I know it is a big step to take, but I have decided to accept Henry's proposal. As you know, I was planning to talk it over some more with you both when I come home for the winter holidays. But since Henry's mother died, he has become more determined to settle on the land as soon as he can. I feel he needs to put down roots and start the life that he has dreamed of for so long. I think he would have been reluctant to leave Hay while his mother was alive, because of her frail health, and no doubt he was her favourite child, as the youngest boy.

His proposal is that he gets the place going (it's been rather run down), and I go on teaching here for the rest of the year. That way I will fulfil my bonded obligation to the department, and I'll be able to save some money towards putting some furniture in the house.

If you both give me your blessing, we will announce our engagement at the end of the month. I will come home for the summer holidays. I want to get married with you there, so would like him to join us after Christmas and we can have a quiet ceremony.

I hope you will come to love him as I have. He has great energy and enthusiasm, and I believe will be a very good farmer. He loves the land and is naturally good with animals, and of course, his work in the stock and station agency has given him a very good understanding of the market and of the best ways of farming in this rather harsh climate.

I will write again soon. I look forward to hearing from you.
My fondest love
Martha

*

With my parents' and his father's blessing, we announce our engagement in late April.

No one is surprised; we've been accepted everywhere from the beginning as destined to marry. It has a fatal inevitability about it, although he has no prospects. A life on the land is what he wants and I want it too, I've decided after a lot of soul-searching, and the place on the river will suit us very well. I lie awake at night and imagine how we can improve the cottage and the garden and plant an orchard and grow our own wheat, once Henry has set up a pump and made irrigation channels in the home paddock.

I put in my resignation and finish the school year in Hay, expecting to marry Henry after Christmas and join him on the place.

*

But Father falls ill, fatally ill, and dies soon after Christmas.

Mother is shocked and silent. Her whole life has revolved around him, around creating a peaceful, well-ordered house that respected his bookish ways, his dedication to his work and need for quiet. He suffered a lot from migraine headaches and would retreat into his study for hours on end. We had to walk around on tiptoe at these times when we were young. If we raised our voices, Mother would emerge from the kitchen where she was baking or the sitting room where she was mending or embroidering, and shush us. At night, Father would leave his shoes outside their bedroom door and it was our job to polish them. At weekends we would help Mother wash, starch and iron his shirts, and brush and press his suit.

He had emigrated from Scotland in his youth when his parents died and went first to the Tobago Islands, where he worked on a sugar cane farm, then to Australia. He came to Wollongong and met Mother and settled here, taking a job as a cadet reporter, riding his bike around the district, getting to know the locals. He rose to become the editor of the *South Coast Times* and a pillar of the community, an elder of the Presbyterian church, a teacher at Sunday school. The staff of the *South Coast Times* and the *Illawarra Mercury* led the funeral procession. Mother and Irene and I were not there; it isn't considered proper for women to be present at funerals. So we sat together in his study and had our own little vigil.

Father was serious and remote. He furnished my mental world

when I was young with stories of the world, of ancient Egypt, of Greek and Roman civilisations, of the Middle Ages, the British Empire, and the making of modern Europe, the origins of the Great War. Together we lived in the house of history and ideas, and as I grew older, we had many conversations about the state of the world.

Henry is interested enough in the world and national events, but hasn't the same depth of knowledge or passion for truth in all its detail. He's interested in politics but only as it affects life on the land, whereas I follow world events with a passion. The highlight of my day is to rise at dawn and read the newspapers, and in the evenings, I do the cryptic crossword.

A few days after the funeral, I enter Father's study, wanting to feel close to him again. It is dark and quiet and smells a little musty. I open the window to let in some fresh air and sit in the leather chair at his desk. It is worn, a little shabby, and I can feel where his legs have rubbed smooth patches in the grain of the leather, and smell something of his presence, a hint of the aromatic pipe tobacco he smoked. I rub my fingers over the worn leather desk pad and open the book that lies on it. It is Gibbons's *History of the Decline and Fall of the Roman Empire, Volume I.*

The first sentence of the first chapter reads, 'In the second century of the Christian era, the empire of Rome comprehended the fairest part of the earth and the most civilised portion of mankind.' Ah, yes; what a decline was there. Father and I often discussed the fall of the empire and reflected on how patterns repeat themselves, as we can see with the British Empire.

I pick up a little book about the Scottish clans with pictures of the different tartans and turn to my father's family name. I read that it can be traced back to Duncan, the Scottish king murdered by Macbeth. Father used to tell us stories of old Scotland and his clan and their loyalty to the royal house of Stewart. One of his ancestors married into a family who produced an English lord, knighted for his discovery of a new way of dyeing cloth. But the old heroic Scotland of the Highland clans was disarmed and destroyed by the English Parliament after the Jacobite Rising of 1745. So our ancestors, as Father often reminded us, lost much of their clan spirit and descended into the middle class. Perhaps that was part of Father's fascination with the decline of the Roman Empire. How the mighty are fallen.

Oh, Father, I wish you were here now so we could have one of our long talks. I was afraid of you when I was little, but when I started to read and think about the world, you would sit me down in the chair under the window, and sit here in this chair, and talk about such topics, and answer my questions. You taught me so much, and I always felt protected and safe with you, I always felt loved. And you taught me how to behave, what makes a good life – respect for one's elders, compassion for those less fortunate, good manners, discretion, loyalty, and honesty. 'Think before you act,' you used to say, and 'Do as you would be done by.'

Life will not be the same without you.

I don't miss the church, the choir, though I did enjoy singing and had my voice trained for a while. I attend church with the family when I visit home but am not now a believer in formal religion. I am not sure there is a God watching over this world. How could an omniscient, rational deity allow humanity to do such things as we have seen, the terrible slaughter and destruction of so many wars, especially the last one? But I don't discuss my doubts with Mother. She has never questioned the Church and has brought us up, like Father, to respect our elders and follow our family traditions.

I cannot imagine her living on her own. Irene and I discuss it and agree that I will postpone going to live on Arendal. I will stay with Mother for this coming year while Irene finishes a posting at Orange, and then she will come home and I will join Henry on the farm.

So Henry and I marry quietly in Wollongong while I am still in mourning, with only my mother and Irene and the old aunties, the spinster sisters who've lived next door all their lives, as witnesses. Henry returns to run the property and I stay on to look after Mother, taking a job at the high school.

I spend the winter holidays with Henry at Arendal. And in the spring holidays, Henry comes to Wollongong. In the last term of the year, I realise I am pregnant, so Irene comes home to look after Mother, and I return to Hay, to the place on the river.

This place

It is hard, much harder than I dreamed it would be. The flock that Henry's father bought to stock the place does not thrive. Drought strikes, and Henry is hand feeding the sheep.

It is a shock to come to this bare little place in the middle of summer. The sun beats down fiercely all day, and often I lie awake till after midnight, waiting for the coolness of dawn. Then as soon as it starts to get light, I get up so I can do my work before the sun starts to heat the house again. On these fierce summer days, cold showers in the open bathroom are a pleasure, but in the winter I will have to heat water in the copper and carry it by the bucketful to the bathing shed if I want to wash in warm water.

Henry's scanty furnishings are a couple of small iron bedsteads and an old cedar chest that was part of the furniture in his childhood home. On hot February afternoons before the furniture comes, I lie on a mattress laid on the living room floor and look out at the bare dry paddocks shimmering in the heat. There is no green barrier between the house and the brown land beyond it. The house is drying up, cracking and shrivelling to a carapace, like the discarded cicada shells on tree trunks and fence posts. I wonder why I left the green and blue of the coast and how long it will take me to dry up till I too become an exoskeleton, a shell of myself on this dusty plain. But I have a child growing inside me so I must stay alive and wait for rain.

A few weeks after my arrival, the furniture – a table and chairs, a sideboard, a cot for the baby, a wardrobe or two, and a couple of old armchairs – I've bought with the little bit of money I'd saved arrives, and the house is less like a camp. We have a car, an old Hupmobile, an

American car, good but heavy on petrol. Sometimes I go into town with Henry, but not always. I notice that he goes fairly often, always on some apparently valid pretext; and he spends a lot of time yarning to the jackeroos at Ulonga, where he goes to buy meat when we don't have a sheep to kill and collect our mail which comes in their bag.

Today, it's evening, the sun has set, and he hasn't come home. I've prepared shepherd's pie with cabbage and peas from the garden. I've lit the lamps and fed the animals, and sit on the veranda watching the night coming down. He should have been home an hour ago. What can have happened, I wonder? Perhaps the pony tripped on a rabbit burrow on the way home and threw him…

I walk out to the east orchard and through the gate, over to the boundary fence, squinting to see in the gathering dusk, straining my ears to hear the horse's hooves. Nothing. Just a shimmer of light on the north-east horizon where the moon is rising, and the calls of the mopoke down in the bend. A rabbit scutters past me, and a fox yelps in the western bend. The dogs answer with a chorus of barks. The baby stirs within me, and I lay my hand on my belly and turn back to the house.

He comes home after dark. He doesn't kiss me as usual but mutters that his stomach is upset and he has to go to the lavatory. I look at his dinner, which I've been keeping warm over a pan of hot water at the back of the stove. Perhaps I should throw it out.

He comes in looking unusually pale.

'Are you all right?'

He groans and rubs his stomach. 'The manager gave me some of his homebrew. He makes his own rum from molasses and sugar. It's potent stuff. I didn't want to drink it, but he insisted.'

'Oh, Henry, you should have just said no. You must have drunk a lot if it made you ill!'

'No,' he groans. 'Just a glassful. I had to be polite.'

'Hmm! Well, I'll put your dinner in the bucket for the dogs in the morning. Next time, Henry, please tell him your wife's waiting for you to come home and have dinner. I'm not used to being on my own at night like this, in the middle of nowhere!'

'I'm sorry, Martha.' He comes over and puts his arms around me, but his breath smells sickly, and I pull away.

Next day, one of the jackeroos from Ulonga comes over late in the afternoon with our newspapers. He swings down from his horse and takes off his hat to greet me, then pulls a bundle of newspapers out of his saddlebag. 'Hello, Mrs Anderson. Is Henry home? He left these behind last night.'

'Oh, thank you. I wondered what happened to them. Would you like a cup of tea?'

'No thanks, ma'am, I have to get back and check on the lambing ewes, make sure they're safe from foxes.' He looks at me for a moment, glances at my swelling belly, then puts on his hat and grins. 'Your hubby's a good poker player! He trashed me last night.'

'Oh, indeed,' I say stiffly. 'Well, thank you for bringing the papers over. I'll tell Henry you came.' I turn and walk back to the house.

I don't say anything about poker to Henry, but store it for future reference. I don't have to wait long.

It's mail day again, and Henry comes home even later this time. I throw out his dinner and wash up. I sit on the veranda in the dark.

I hear his footsteps, the screen door closing, the kitchen tap running, and call, 'Henry! I'm out here.'

His face is in the shadows, I can't read his expression.

'I'm sorry, Martha,' he mumbles, 'the manager wanted to talk to me about his latest breeding experiments, crossing merinos with that wrinkly breed. He reckons they'll bear more wool.'

'Henry,' I say tiredly, 'don't give me more excuses. I can smell the rum. You've been drinking and playing cards again. Don't lie to me.'

The first time I was prepared to believe that he didn't want to offend the manager, that he may have just had a glass or two more than he admitted. But now I know that he's telling downright lies, that he uses these visits to escape the place and his duties for a while.

'Next time,' I say, 'don't bother to come home. You may as well spend the night there. But I may not be here when you do come back.'

'Huh!' he scoffs. 'You wouldn't get far in your condition. Anyway, a man has to have a bit of company sometimes.'

'Am I not company enough?'

I am genuinely puzzled, as I am not discontented with just the two of us here. I have my thoughts while I am working and when work is done I sit and read the paper or one of my books. Or I listen to the wireless if there is a concert on, or the cricket on summer days, while I mend Henry's socks and knit jumpers for our winter baby. The winters here are as cold as the summers are hot; Henry says there is often frost on the grass, and any puddles of rain freeze over.

Of course, I enjoy intelligent conversation with like-minded people, but mostly my own thoughts are company enough, and conversations with Henry about the land, the pastures, the lambing ewes, his ideas for breeding for fine wool. And the events that are happening in the world, the latest reports from overseas. On the news this morning, they said that Trotsky has been expelled from the Communist party, and Josef Stalin has taken control. China has been attacking British and American ships, and British warships have attacked and disabled their gun batteries. I worry when I think of what will become of the world if Communism takes over in China as well as Russia. Mao Zedong is leading a peasant uprising against their landlords in China. Who knows where that will lead. No doubt the peasants have been greatly oppressed, but once revolution starts, history teaches, events get out of control, power goes to the new leaders' heads, and the new regime may be worse than the old.

I rise from my reverie. He's sitting smoking, staring out at the shadows of the cedar on the moonlit lawn.

'Just don't lie to me again, Henry. I can't live with a man who lies. I don't like drinking and gambling either, or time wasting, but the worst thing you can do is to lie to me.'

I walk outside for a last visit to the lavatory before bed.

*

When the fierce heat abates, I begin to feel kinder towards the little house and to take an interest in the garden. Henry is careful to come home for the evening meal now when he's done his business in town or at Ulonga. I'm getting heavy and slow, and he's helping a lot more, cleaning out the fireplaces and laying the fires for me in the mornings before he sets off for the paddocks, and scrubbing the floors once a week so I don't have to get down on my hands and knees.

He establishes the front lawn and plants the privet hedge around it. As it grows, he clips it into battlement formation. In the centre of the lawn is the cedar tree, the saving grace of the place, already tall and stately. Henry says it owes its shape to the children of the couple who lived here before. They used to climb on it when it was a young sapling and broke down all but the central growth. It saves the house from the worst of the sun's heat, for it spreads out like a giant umbrella over the whole house. In winter the branches will be bare of leaf, bearing sprays of bright mustard-yellow berries, which will shrivel and drop. The parrots love them, but the children will have to be taught not to eat them, for they are toxic to humans. In spring, it will be covered in bright green leaf and clusters of delicate lilac-pink flowers filling the air with a musky perfume.

We spend evenings in the lamplight planning the back garden for flowers and vegetables and poring over Hazlewood's catalogue to choose trees and shrubs. The citrus orchard was already established when Henry came here and flourishes because it is regularly watered. Henry digs drains through the citrus trees and around the hedge to the orchard on the eastern side of the house, where he plants apple (Jonathan and Granny Smith), peach, pear, apricot, quince, almond and mulberry trees. I acquire a Fowlers preserving pan and jars and, once the peach and apricot trees are established, they will keep us in bottled fruit for the year.

I sit by the fire on chilly autumn evenings, dreaming of life ahead, of the baby to be born in a few weeks' time…will it be a boy or a girl? I hope for a boy. I think Henry would like that too, for our eldest.

New beginnings

How comical it is to see Henry setting off on foot to do some job near the house, followed in single file by all the animals that have been here with him from the beginning – two dogs, a cat, a pet lamb and a rooster. One of his dogs is a dear little fellow named Pompey, who is very jealous of me.

There's a very lovable little kitten which follows us everywhere, and one evening we go for a walk in the Ulonga paddock next to us. A bull which is grazing there begins to paw the ground and bellow, then comes towards us, so we run as fast as we can across the rough surface of the ploughed firebreak. Henry carries the kitten, but it scrambles down and runs away. It's some days before it comes back home, and when it does, we don't like it nearly so much; it clings and whines. One day it goes bush.

I love it when the galahs fly above the gum trees where they roost in the evenings, swooping in formation, swirls of pink and grey, calling to each other, then circling in to the branches, squabbling and jostling like a big family of unruly children. Their babies cry all through the hot summer days, rasping in a monotonous insatiable complaint while their parents seek food for them. They annoyed me at first, but now when I rest in the afternoons on the veranda, their dirge lulls me into a dreamlike state.

David is born in July 1927, a big handsome blond baby. I delight in him, my firstborn. He is all sunshine and milky smells, and when he sleeps, he snuffles and sometimes mews like a kitten. Soon he is smiling and chuckling, and Henry sits with him on his lap when he comes home from the paddocks and plays 'this little piggy' and 'round and round the garden' with him till he gets hiccups from laughing so much and I have to take him and give him another feed to settle him.

Mother comes to stay with us when he is three months old, and stays for three months, but she has no experience of inland heat and develops a goitre, so has to return to the coast.

Mother and Irene pay for me to bring David down to Sydney for a holiday with them in the summer. By now he is sitting up, and his favourite greeting to people is to draw himself up and growl in an amicable way, by way of saying 'Me heap big chief!' One day, he is sitting on the table when the people next door visit. He growls to greet the little boy of three, who responds by hiding his face in his grandmother's skirts and saying, 'Lion, Nana, baby lion!' much to our amusement.

I am able to take a couple of trips into town alone and feel wonderfully free as I walk the city streets, stop for a cup of tea and a scone, and buy some material to make clothes for David, who is growing so fast, and for some new summer dresses for me. I wonder if I will ever feel this way again. But still, I'm glad to go home. I miss the space, the quiet, the birds in the morning, the river, the night sounds.

*

I am beginning to feel this is my place, but I still have fits of discontent. Today, Henry tells me he's going into town to pick up some supplies.

'But Henry, you went five days ago! What do you need so urgently? I think it would be better to have a regular day for town, no more than once a week. There's so much to do here.'

'I need some parts for the tractor.'

'But you were using it yesterday. You said you were going to have all the channels dug and the pump working before the worst of summer, and they're only half done!'

'Yes, but the tractor's cooling system isn't working well. It needs some new parts.'

'What about the generator?' I say. 'You promised me we'd have power for lights in the house before David was born. He's nearly a year old now, and the generator only worked for about three months before it broke down. Have you ordered a part for it?'

'Yeah, but they're out of stock. Anyway, what's wrong with lamplight?'

'Oh, it's all very well for you. You can just take off in the mornings and go out in the paddocks, and leave me to keep the house going, to cook the meals, to keep things clean, to look after David, to wash and iron, in conditions that my mother would think are nineteenth century!'

'Well, this is the outback, my dear, and I never told you it would be like city life.'

'And you promised me you'd grow wheat so I could grind flour and make our own bread. You promised a cow so we could have fresh milk and cream and butter. It's not just you any more, Henry, batching and living rough. You have a family, you have to make this place work so we can live decently and raise healthy, well fed, well bred children.'

He turns away, his face red, his eyes puckered, picks up his hat and strides towards the door. 'I should have known not to marry a city girl!'

'Oh, go!' I say, my voice cracking. 'Go into town, hang around yarning in the pub, wasting time. Meantime, I'll get on with my work!'

*

When David begins to walk but is still having daytime sleeps, he sometimes will wake up, scramble out of his cot and sneak off – I can see the little figure toddling over to where Henry is working. He loves to be with Henry, and soon is going out in the paddocks with him. Sometimes he comes home proudly holding the reins, really doing the driving. Our cot is a heavy oak one with one slat missing, and once, soon after he began walking, we went out to the veranda in response to his cries to find him stuck in the gap.

'Ha ha!' laughed Henry. 'He's forgotten to allow for his big end!'

But it wasn't long before he was climbing over the sides. Although he is adventurous and determined, like his grandfather and father he is excessively safety-conscious and will watch the car door to see that it is properly shut. 'At not too safe,' he will say about something, 'not too safe at all.' We have one wobbly chair in the kitchen, and he will rush to stop visitors from sitting on it. 'At chair fa' over,' he warns them.

When he was born, the Red Cross was using the old gaol for a maternity home, so it has become a family joke that he was born in a gaol.

When he is twenty months old, the doctor confirms I am pregnant again. This will be our last child, I think, though I don't say so to Henry, who wants a family of five children like his own. But I find the pregnancies so hard in these conditions, especially through the hot summer; and I want our children to have a good upbringing and education. The seasons here are unforgiving, and we never know if there will be enough rain to give good feed for the sheep, whether the wool crop will be good or wool prices will be favourable, whether we can sell enough wethers at the market at a good price to carry on for another year. We have nothing to fall back on, no reserves. And we can't borrow any more money from Henry's father.

Vera is born in March 1929 in the new maternity hospital they have established in a big old house in Hay. Mysteriously, I contract scarlet fever when she is a few days old, and we are moved over to the isolation ward of the general hospital. A sister from the maternity hospital comes over to nurse us. Scarlet fever cases have to be isolated until all peeling has stopped, which means eight weeks in hospital.

To stay sane while I am incarcerated, I get Henry to buy me some material, and make myself, by hand, an over-blouse of some light cream woollen stuff, and a pleated viyella skirt on a lawn top, in a grey and rose check.

In the next room, there is a ten-year-old boy from Booligal, who starts talking to himself, poor little chap. 'I'm cold, I am,' I hear him saying to himself when he is out on the veranda, 'I'm going inside.' He doesn't have many visitors.

I'm not allowed visitors, so when Henry comes to town once or twice a week, he stands with David in his arms just outside the door of my ward, and they wave to me and blow kisses. David seems to accept that I am a prisoner, and Henry writes me letters about David's latest adventures, the new words he is saying, and how the sheep are going, how many have had lambs after good winter rains. So I feel hopeful of new beginnings, a new season and better times.

It is such a relief to come home again. Our little house seems like a palace after being confined to one room for so long. But David treats me like a stranger at first and will only let his father bathe him and put him to bed, and insists on being outside with him whenever he can. In a way, it's a relief, as I can focus on nursing Vera, a fussy feeder, and getting the housework done between feeds.

Because the skin on my legs is still peeling, I don't use the bath, but sponge myself in a dish I keep for the purpose and wear stockings day and night until the peeling stops.

As for Vera, David is suspicious of her at first and says, 'Mamma, when're you takin' 'er back to 'ospital?' He glares at her and growls, and once or twice I've caught him poking her in the stomach when she is crying.

No wonder he is jealous. She is greatly troubled by indigestion and it takes me hours to feed her. Hard to get my chores done, hard to listen to her crying when I have to put her down. But she is a very pretty baby, and an active one, walking earlier than David did. Henry adores her and I have to remind him not to pay her too much attention and make David even more jealous.

Once she can walk, David starts to warm to her, and leads her outside, showing her some of his favourite spots in the garden – the cedar tree, where he climbs up to the first branch and encourages her to follow, the grape arbor outside the kitchen, the rich soil where Henry digs in the kitchen compost, the earthworms that wriggle away when David pokes the earth with a stick.

They fight often, and once Vera threw a tomahawk at David and cut his forehead, fortunately, a glancing blow. No doubt he did something mean to her, but I did not see, so all I could do was console him and bathe the cut, and give them both a talking to about playing together and being kind to each other. Often they play together very happily, and with great accord. They might be playing some absorbing game, and stop as if they have a silent agreement to carry into the kitchen the firewood which Henry has neatly piled at the back door.

When it is laundry day, the children play near me while I boil the copper, wring out and rinse the clothes, rinse and wring them again with the mangle, then hang them on the line. They play with the pegs, turn the handle of the mangle sometimes, and hand the pegs to me when I am hanging out the clothes. It is hard work, made harder by the fact that Henry has put the clothesline down at the bottom of the garden, so I have to carry the heavy wet clothes down there to hang them. The laundry was another shed built under the tank near the house. But the shed and its contents (it was our storage room) were burnt down.

One day, I was boiling clothes in the copper when I saw Henry entering the home paddock in the sulky, back from his morning round of the paddocks. I hurriedly stoked the copper fire and took the children in with me to get lunch.

'Whassat noise, Mamma?' David asked.

We stopped eating and became aware of crackling and the smell of smoke. We rushed out, but could only look on helplessly. I'd left the door of the fireplace ajar, and coals must have fallen onto the kindling on the floor in front of it so it caught alight. Everything is so dried out by the summer heat that the fire took just a few minutes to destroy the shed.

For a few days after that, Vera and David play fire, rushing in to where I am, crying, 'Moke, Mamma, moke! Big fire!'

I scold them and tell them to play another game.

Henry takes it stoically, but makes no effort to replace the shed, and is not above reminding me of how I burnt the laundry down.

I inherit some money from a cousin's estate and use most of it to extend the house. We have a kitchen and bathroom added to the western end; Henry had already taken down the partition between living room and the old kitchen to make one long living room with fireplaces at each end. We have the verandas, already gauzed in, enclosed in louvres, and that makes the house more liveable. We even have a chip heater in the bathroom, so no more cold showers. The saving features of the house are the long living room and the enclosed verandas, for which Henry has made canvas blinds on my treadle Singer. That enables us to manage with only two bedrooms, one for each of us, which we share as dressing rooms, he with the little boy, I with the little girl. I am quite sure I couldn't bear sharing either a bedroom or a bed with him. I made this clear from the beginning. I need my privacy.

When I first told him, in those early days when we had only rudimentary furniture, he said, 'Oh, Martha…but we're a married couple, we're not divorced!'

'Yes, Henry,' I replied. 'And I do love you, but I don't wish to share a bed with you. I need my sleep, and in any case, I think it's better not to be tempted too often.'

'Tempted?' He said, looking at me quizzically. 'Isn't it proper for a man to make love to his wife?'

'Of course it is. But Henry…we have so little to spare, we can't afford to have too many children, and life out here is so hard physically. There are no reliable means of birth control that I know of, other than using the safe times of the month. We've already proven we're a fertile couple. Besides, I need my privacy. I don't want to be dressing and undressing in front of you.'

'Hmm.' He looked down at his hand and shrugged. 'But Martha… a man has urges, you know, and I will find it hard.'

'Well, Henry, I don't know what to suggest. Hard work and self-discipline are good medicine for physical desire.'

'Hard work! Strewth, woman, I can't work when I'm sleeping!' He laughed and reached out to me. 'I'd just like to hold you sometimes, to cuddle you, to kiss you.'

I didn't respond to his touch. 'Well, one thing leads to another. I am as I am, and we both need to be mature about this.'

'Oh, mature, is it? Well, you're older than me!' He tossed his head and turned to go out the door.

'That was uncalled for!'

He slammed the door behind him.

We were cold to each other for a while, but he soon got over it.

I do fret about it sometimes, knowing it's hard for him. But I won't give in. He has to accept that we only come together at safe times. Self-control is what makes humans different from animals. I don't want to get pregnant again. I know he wants a big family, like his own, but I am happy with our pigeon pair, and it is all we can do to raise them properly.

With the rest of my cousin's money, I buy our first new car, a Vauxhall. I tell Henry that now I will hear no more of the burnt laundry, and he knows he's struck rock.

Hay days

My hopes for better times are dashed. Things get even harder after Vera's birth, what with the recurring droughts and the worsening state of the economy. The American stock market crashed in October last year when Vera was six months old, and in Australia, this year the unemployment rate has risen to twenty-one per cent. We haven't had a good season since Henry took up the lease here, and the long-term forecasts are bleak. They talk of a nineteen-year drought cycle. Since the bad seasons started about the time we came here, at this rate, we can't expect much relief before 1945. I wonder if we'll hold out that long.

Henry comes home in the evening, his face dark, and tells me how many sheep he has found dead. He moves them all to the home paddock and feeds them by hand, but they are so skinny, in such poor condition, they might as well be dead. In the end, he gets a shotgun and finishes off the last of them. That night, he doesn't touch his dinner.

'It was no use trying to save them, Martha. Kinder to finish them off quickly.' He rolls a cigarette and sits staring out at the shadows cast by the cedar tree in the moonlight.

'Henry, I've been thinking. We can't stay on here with no income. The drought will break sooner or later, but may not till next winter now. I'll have to take the children with me and go back to teaching for a while.'

'Oh, Martha, I suppose you're right. I could keep things going here, and maybe I can get work jackerooing on Ulonga. They're big enough to keep feeding their sheep, to sit it out, and they still need workers to keep them going.'

I go to see the headmaster, and he is glad to take me on again.

'I haven't had a satisfactory replacement for you,' he says, slicking back his hair with that familiar gesture. 'Most of the young teachers I get don't last long. They just don't have the stamina for inland life. And it so happens that our senior school teacher is leaving at the end of this term.'

So in 1930, I start there again at the beginning of the year. Henry's father lets me have the back flat in his house, which is very comfortable; just as he did with his leasehold property, Mr Anderson has spared no expense in fitting the place out well. He has finally agreed to let Florence start nursing, so she is not here any more. He is going to Adelaide to live with Henry's eldest brother and his family and has a middle-aged couple living in the front flat. It is such a pleasure to have electricity, a proper bathroom with hot and cold running water, a flush toilet attached to the house, a septic tank (no more smelly outdoor lavatory!) and a kitchen with an Aga stove that doesn't have to be stoked up all the time, and has a warming cupboard and a good big oven. I rise early to give the children breakfast, stoke up the stove and get ready for the day.

I've found a maid to come in during the day to do the chores and look after the children. Rita is a little nuggety girl, pure gold. She is not only quick, deft and clean, but she is very good with the children. She comes before I leave in the morning, and stays until I get home, which is as quickly as I can in the afternoon. She has weekends to herself, and I always do the washing and ironing on Saturdays.

But J.T. Lang is in power in New South Wales, mounted on his financial hobby horse and riding a wild course. His plan to combat the Depression is to withdraw all the state funds from government bank accounts and hold them at Trades Hall in cash so the federal government can't access the money, to inject more funds into revitalising industry and commerce, to spend more and increase government debt.

Every payday, our cheques seem to be smaller, and actually are from time to time, so I am finding it very hard to keep us going. The rent of the flat, small as it is, becomes too much, so I decide the only honest thing to do is to find somewhere cheaper. I arrange to rent two rooms with shared use of the kitchen and bathroom – how hard it will be to bear! – from a young married woman in this street.

But I have reckoned without Mr Anderson. I write to tell him of my decision and get this reply.

> Dear Martha
>
> Please don't consider moving out. I know how hard things are, and I want you and the children to be as comfortable and safe as you can be while you are teaching.
>
> Let us hope the terrible Depression will be over soon.
>
> I am not relying on a certain figure from the Hay house to make ends meet, and it is no hardship for me. From now on, just pay me what you can afford.
>
> I hope Henry is working hard and doing his bit to keep you all afloat.
>
> I am well, apart from a flare up of my arthritis in the cold weather. The winds here are very cutting, they come straight off the Antarctic. But I am determined to finish installing an off-peak hot water system here.
>
> Write again when you have time and let me know how you are going. Hugs for the children.
> Affectionately
> George Anderson

But I have to cut down on the maid's services. She agrees to look after Vera at her mother's house during school hours, for by this time David is a pupil in the crowded kindergarten.

Of course, this reckless course of Lang's leaves the government flat on its back, unable to pay its public servants and forced to close the Savings Bank. Who knows if I will get my next pay cheque.

As for Henry, he is supposed to be using this time to finish some of the improvements he's started. He's built a bigger shed on the riverbank to house the machinery and stock feed and the vehicle when we have one. He's in the process of building a proper shearing shed to replace the small one that was there when we took the place, with an engine room and pens at the back, a loading bay, and yards for the sheep. But he stopped work on it when we lost our flock. He says he will finish it when he has time and the money to buy more materials, but I do wonder. He appears on Friday afternoon, saying he will return to Arendal on Monday morning. But each morning and afternoon until Wednesday afternoon at the earliest, he finds urgent reasons for going downtown, where he idles the hours away in endless yarning. Needless to say, people gossip about his leaving the breadwinner's duty to me, and I am concerned, not for us but for him; I can't stand the worry of seeing him so feckless.

After a couple of months of drifting, he doesn't appear on Friday as usual but turns up on Saturday afternoon. He greets me with a hug and picks the children up in turn and swings them around till they squeal with delight.

'Henry, where have you been? What has happened?'

'Good news, Martha! I've got a job on Ulonga. One of the jackeroos took ill and has gone back to his family, so I started this week. I'll sleep over there during the week and come in on Saturdays, go back Sunday evening.'

He brings a leg of Ulonga hogget and some vegetables from the garden there, and we celebrate with roast dinner and a glass or two of home-brewed beer.

I have missed him and, of course, he has missed me. He is always hungry for physical contact with me, and I ration it as much as I can. Tonight, though, I yield to the happiness of being together, and to his good news, and put my fears aside. When he enters me, I shudder and let go, and soon we move in unison, and I start to spasm and cry, 'Oh God!' As I lie afterwards with his head pillowed on my breast, I know that we are meant to be together, that this is the secret of our bond, this and our dream of life on the land. Whatever happens, I know that Arendal is our place, this place we know.

Now, each weekend we have a happy day and a half together and are separately busy during the week. I wish sometimes that we could go on like this, with me working in the department and him jackerooing, but of course, we have to make a go of our place as soon as the seasons turn better. I love teaching, and he is not unhappy working for someone else, and I have no anxiety about him, or about whether the ewes will have a good lambing season, whether there will be enough winter rain, whether the wool prices will enable us to continue for another year. Now at least we both have an income, even though there are uncertainties about how long the department will be able to keep paying its teachers.

*

Every afternoon after school, if it's not raining, I take David and Vera out to the park in cooler weather, and to the river in summer. The park is spacious and shady, with swings and see-saws and plenty of green lawn. It is kept by a local character called Les Parr, who not only works very hard in its care but is a most amusing conversationalist, much quoted.

Les is a happy man; he loves his work and has a free hand to improve the garden beds with seasonal plantings and add to the rose bushes and shrubs when there is a gap. He has a cottage at the western edge of the park, almost lost to sight amid its garden and hedge. He is self-respecting and highly respected. I can't think of anyone more typical of the Australian working man at his best. I've got to know him well because the school takes up one corner of the park, and I walk the shady paths four times a day on my way to and from work, besides taking the children there in the afternoons after school.

This afternoon, Les was busy raking the leaves on the pathway around the swings. This is David and Vera's favourite place, and we spend most of our park time here. There are two swings, side by side; I always put Vera on the one closer to the ground, which is covered with soft sand, and David on the higher one. David can push himself, loves to fly as high as he can, but Vera needs me in attendance.

'Push, Mamma, push! Me go highest, up to the sky!'

It has a gentle rhythm, my pushes, her swings, but gets rather monotonous, so I'm happy to chat with Les while I keep her moving.

'Tell me what your life was like, Les, when you were little.'

'Ah, Mrs Anderson, there was never a dull moment. We lived on the common, permanent like, in a hut with dirt floors, but it was snug enough in the winter with the fire goin'. Bloomin' 'ot in the summer, though! But we had a big pepper tree near us, and Mum'd sit under it and do 'er mendin' while us kids played with jacks made from knuckle bones or marbles we'd traded with other kids.'

'What were the other people living there like? Were they rough?' I asked as I gave Vera another big push.

'Nay, they wasn't too bad. Might kick up a shindig sometimes when they hadda bit o' money to spare for drinkin', but everyone looked out for each other. There was drovers, stockmen, tinkers, road workers like me dad, a few tramps'd come and go.'

'Did you have other family living in the town?' I asked, as I picked Vera up from the sand under the swing, dusted her off and set her moving again.

'Nay, Dad'd come from Victoria, and Mum's rellies lived in Balranald, further down the river. But I remember they come to visit one time, and stayed for tea. Mum cooked a couple o' rabbits; she made a good stew, with a few greens she scrounged from the greengrocer and dandelions from around the common. When she 'ad the stew ready, she got out these bits of cloth and put 'em on the table. "Eh, Mum," me little brother Ricky piped up, "what's these little towels for?" Mum gave 'im one of 'er 'ard looks, and showed 'im how to tuck it into 'is shirt. "It's to keep yer clothes clean, silly!"'

I laughed. 'Vera and David, it's time to go home now and have tea. Last six swings! One, two…'

Les leaned on his rake and gazed across the lawns, chuckling. 'Our hut was just one room, and we slept on bags on the floor. We was used to it. But the rellies wouldn't go that night, they was still talkin' and drinkin' cups of tea, and we was all half asleep. Me big brother Ned'd had enough. He pipes up, "Hey Mum, where's them bags?"'

'Oh, poor woman. What did she do?'

'She went red and tried to laugh it off. I think her rellies lived in a proper house. But we was always clean, and Mum always put food on the table.'

*

This winter there is an epidemic of mumps at the government hostel for boys on the park's southern boundary. The hostel is quarantined, and the two young resident masters must be at their wits' end to keep the boys busy. But lately, when we go to the park in the afternoons, the boys are roaming all over.

Today, I protested to one of the masters. 'Mr Small, are you aware that mumps is supposed to be contagious at sixteen feet?' I said, as I pulled Vera close to me and called David back from a game of chasings he was gravitating towards.

'Mrs Anderson, you try keeping twenty-odd young lads cooped up within doors and fences for weeks at a time!' He turned away and strode off to round up the strays.

I shepherded my pair back to the swings, a bit ashamed of how selfish I must sound to a harassed young housemaster.

Soon, with the shrinking pay cheque, I am forced to stop paying Rita to mind Vera during the day, and persuade the kindergarten to take her even though she doesn't turn five until next year. My greatest fear is that one of the children will get some infectious disease and have to go to the hospital's isolation ward; but the worst thing that happens is David's heavy colds. When he gets sick, I have to leave him well rugged up on a daybed on the veranda, with books and puzzles and something to eat and drink, and rely on our kindly neighbour to give him lunch and keep an eye on him. I give her a little money, and when Henry brings mutton or hogget and vegetables in from Ulonga, I share it with her. These are anxious days.

There are many men without work in town, and the government gives them ration vouchers they can use to buy food and tobacco. They do odd jobs around town, sweeping the streets, clearing the gutters in exchange. Some of them do roadwork, which is subsidised with federal funds, but there is always a queue outside the shire office for work at the start of a week, and not many are taken on.

When I do my weekly shopping at the grocer's and cash my government cheque, the shopkeeper leans over the counter and whispers, 'Don't let those poor devils see it, Mrs Anderson!'

The Sussos, they're called, slang for Sustenance men. More and more tents and swags are popping up on the common, and their children come to school looking ragged and unwashed. I am fortunate to have work, to have a roof over our heads. Whenever I have a little change in my purse, I give some to them, even a few pence. Unemployment is at an all-time high; twenty-nine per cent is the latest figure. Henry says the swaggies are turning up at Ulonga almost every day now. Poor things, what future do they have? A life on the road, walking from station to station, doing odd jobs where they can, scrounging for a sandwich and a cup of tea, and, if they're lucky, a bit of change. They mostly give our place a miss, as they know on the grapevine it's lean pickings there.

At last, at the beginning of 1934, things improve enough in the economy and in the seasons for me to bring the children home. Henry has saved enough to buy a new flock of young ewes, and mates them with the Ulonga stud rams, in exchange for helping them harvest the wheat in their home paddock. He expects a good lambing, and there's been good winter rain.

But I am pregnant again, which I have mixed feelings about.

A mother's love

Malcolm is born at the start of summer, November 1934. He is a bonny, healthy baby with brown hair and hazel eyes like mine – none of our children have Henry's lovely blue eyes – and is soon smiling and gurgling. But Mother has been ill and I am concerned about her, so in the summer holidays, I use some of the money I managed to put aside when teaching to take the children with me to Wollongong.

Mother's house is weatherboard lined with pine, and it has to be relined because it has been invaded by borers from the pittosporum tree in the garden. The order for the work was given some months ago, but the builders have only just started when we get there.

The first day we arrive, I see how strained and unwell she is, and when the children are playing outside, I make a pot of tea and sit down with her on the veranda.

'Mother, let me find somewhere nearby for us to stay while the work is being done. It's too much for you, with all this noise and dust, to have three little children sharing the space.'

Mother pats my hand and takes a sip of tea. 'No, no, dear. I won't hear of it. The children can play outside, and you can take them to the park or down to the beach each day. Who knows when I'll see you all again?' She sighs and leans back in her chair, eyes shut.

She looks old, much older than last time I saw her. Her skin is grey, and there's a bluish tinge around her mouth.

It is chaotic, with the workmen hammering and sawing, dust everywhere, and no matter how much Irene and I dust and sweep at the end of the day, there is always a fine coating on things. I take the children out each day to the shops or to the beach or the park, but they are restless and noisy, and some days it's raining and they can't play outside. Mother has a chronic cough, which has got worse, and even if we close off her sitting room, the dust still gets in.

A few days after we arrive, when the workmen are tearing out the lining in the kitchen and the house is full of noise and dust, Mother takes to her bed feeling sick and weak, and doesn't get up again. Next morning I take in her usual early morning cup of tea, expecting to see her sitting up waiting for me as usual. But she's still asleep, soundly it seems, lying on her back.

'Good morning, Mother. Here's your cup of tea.'

She doesn't stir. I touch her hand. Her skin is cold, there is no pulse of life, no response to my touch. Her hands are resting on top of the covers, her face peaceful.

I turn away and call for Irene. I can't bear to look at her. I am not ready for this. She should not die now, it is too soon, we didn't know she was dying, we might have been able to prevent it. I just wanted to spend some time with her and help her to get well again, to carry on her quiet, unassuming life, to get to know her grandchildren a little better. I wanted to share with her what is happening on the place, what changes we've made, what our hopes and plans are.

I feel so guilty. Had I not come and added to her worries, to the noise and chaos, she might have survived and lived a few more years. I am her eldest child, I should have been looking after her.

The funeral is small; just the family and the old aunties from next door and some elderly members of the Presbyterian congregation present. I weep all through the funeral. I feel my old life has come to an end.

No one will ever love you like your mother, will understand you, care for you, sacrifice herself for you, want only the best for you. No man can love like this.

I wish that I had stayed in the domestic circle like Irene and not gone off to the outback and started a new life. Not got married. At least I could have kept Mother company in her widowed years.

But then, I would not know Arendal or the river or Henry, whom I still love with all his faults, and I would not have these three beautiful children.

In my childhood, Mother was the figure we all took for granted, in the background sewing, cooking, cleaning and polishing, wearing an apron except when she sat down to a meal. She used to change out of her day clothes in the evening before dinner, and always set the table nicely, with flowers and a candle. She saw the home, I think, as a sanctuary from the outside world, and her main focus was to shelter her husband from the stresses and pressures of his work when he was at home, and to bring us up to respect him, the home and the family. For her, he was the head of the household, the one around whom everything revolved.

My own experience of marriage so far falls short of the model she set. I believe that the man should be the head of the household and be honoured and cared for. Yet I struggle with this, much as I love Henry. I am beginning to wonder if he is a flash in the pan – full of enthusiasm and passion at the start of something, too ready to give up when things don't go well.

But Mother – she was always just there. As I grew up, she was ready with a kind word and a cup of tea if I was tired, always there to listen to my worries. Now she is gone, returned to the earth, and the house echoes with emptiness.

Irene and I have little to say to each other. I think we are both numb.

It's all the worse for the workmen's presence. They downed tools for a few days in respect, but the marks of their work are everywhere, and the usual order and cleanliness that Mother preserved is just a memory.

Sometimes I catch myself looking up and expecting to see Mother sitting in her armchair knitting, or nursing one of the children, and see only an empty space.

To make things worse, Malcolm gets croup a few days after the funeral. He is not quite six months old. It came on very suddenly in the morning and, by night time, he is struggling for breath. I sit with him in the bathroom with door and window shut, running the hot water, trying to help him to breathe. His breathing is getting worse, each in-breath harsh and rasping, and he is turning blue around the mouth. I fear that he is dying. I will wake Irene and send her out to rouse the doctor who lives in our street.

As I stand up, holding Malcolm up to my shoulder, patting him on the back to try and help him clear his airway, I hear Mother's voice, saying, 'There's a bottle of ipecac in the bathroom cupboard. Give him a quarter of a teaspoonful every half hour to help him bring up the plug of mucus that's choking his airway.'

I've never heard of this remedy before, but I do it, praying that it won't poison him. After the second dose, his chest heaves and he coughs up a gob of phlegm. His colour and breathing return to normal and he settles to sleep in my arms. I say a prayer, a genuine one, and thank Mother for looking after us and saving Malcolm's life. I haven't prayed like this since I was a child.

This changes my idea of death. I believe that the end of physical life means that a person's spirit goes into another realm entirely, but I've never been convinced of the Christian idea of heaven and hell. But now I think that our spirits live on for a time, not in physical form but in a state that means we are still aware of the world we have lost and our loved ones in it. So I feel less alone. I know Mother is still with us, watching over us, that she still cares.

Disaster strikes again

'Malcolm, it's bath time,' I call.

'No tanks, Mum. I hadda bath yesserday,' he yells back. Yesterday it was 'No tanks, Mum. I had one last week.'

'Malcolm, come and get some clothes on,' I say later, when he is playing naked under the grape arbor, making hills and roadways in the red dirt.

'No tanks, Mum. A man doesn't need clothes.'

After lunch, a car turns into our home paddock, and Malcolm rushes out to see who it is. Before I can get there, a man has stepped out and speaks to Malcolm.

'Hello, young feller. What place is this?'

Malcolm looks at the shiny new car, eyes wide, then turns to the man. 'Hello, mister. This is 'Stralia. Can I come for a drive in your car?'

When he is three years old, in 1937, Simon is born, a late January baby. I swear this will be our last child. I am forty-two now; surely this must be the last pregnancy I will have to bear through the summer heat. He is an eager, active baby, walking before he can talk, talking before he has words, making up his own language, babbling away nineteen to the dozen when he is not asleep or eating. He follows Malcolm everywhere, and together they get up to even more mischief – tying a tin can to the cat's back leg, putting prickles in David's bed, pouring a bottle of India ink over the blanket on Malcolm's bed, throwing Vera's drawings into the fire…

It's all a bit much for me, having to supervise correspondence lessons for the older children and keep an eye on the little ones. To make things harder, the seasons turn bad again and Henry is hand feeding the sheep. Great cracks open in the earth, the river shrinks to pools connected by sandbars, and the house tank is only half full. There is no water to spare for the garden, and we have to buy our vegetables from the Chinese gardener at Ulonga.

Today there is a dark cloud on the horizon and I pray that it is bringing rain. But it is approaching too fast. The sky darkens, the wind howls through the trees, and the birds fall quiet, even the galahs. The dogs howl in their kennels. Henry is out in the paddocks somewhere. I hope he finds shelter. I've heard of these giant dust storms, bringing the red soil from the arid regions inland. Men and beasts have died in them. I call the children inside, wet some tea towels, and we close all the doors and the louvres on the verandas and sit in the living room on the rug, holding our breath as the wind howls around the house. The dust comes in through the cracks in the walls and swirls around us. The little boys cry and hide their faces in my skirts. Vera sits huddled beside me, trying to hide under my arm.

Only David is not afraid. He holds his hand in front of his face and says, 'Huh! I can't see my hand! Look, no hands!'

It is as dark as night time when the lamps are out. I kneel forward to feel for a basin I had placed near us, with water and face cloths in it.

Vera shrieks and buries her face in a cushion.

'Children, here's a wet cloth for each of you. Hold it over your face till the storm passes. You can breathe through it safely, and it will keep the grit out of your eyes and nose and mouth.'

I feel around for each of them and press a cloth into their hands. Then I settle back with one over my face, breathing slowly, keeping my mind quiet by reciting the opening lines of Virgil's first *Eclogue* under my breath.

> *Tityre, tu patulae recubans sub tegmine fagi*
> *siluestrem tenui Musam meditaris auena.*
> (Tityrus, you lie beneath spread of sheltering beech
> Studying the woodland Muse on a thin oat-straw.)

*

When the storm has passed, there are inches of dust over everything.

Towards evening, Henry rides home, the pony stumbling through the soft red dirt, his head down, no longer chestnut, an unnatural copper red.

Malcolm rushes up to them. 'Dad! Dad! Where you been? It was scary here! We couldn't see anything!'

A red-stained handkerchief veils the lower part of Henry's face and his hands and neck are caked with red dust. Under his hat, his eyes are piercingly blue. His clothes are a dirty rusty colour.

As he gives the pony a drink of water from the tank and curry-combs him to get off some of the caked dust, he tells me what happened. 'I was out in the far paddock over the railway line when it hit. We sheltered in an old hut until the worst of it was over. But, Martha…' His voice tails off and he wipes his hand across his eyes, making his eyes even more piercing in his dark face.

'What, Henry? What is it?'

'Our boundary fence with Ulonga is covered over, and not many of the sheep are left. Only the ones in the bottom paddock near the bend. I've put them in the top paddock where the fence is OK. But I reckon over a thousand sheep are buried under red dust. They gathered at the fence to try to shelter. I spent a couple of hours cleaning out the troughs so that the ones left can get water. But – it's a disaster – I don't see how we can carry on.'

I put my arms around him and hold him as we sway together gently, sharing our grief.

Moments pass, then I release him and take his hand. 'We'll survive, Henry. We always do. We'll find a way to restock. This will pass.'

He sighs and turns back to combing the pony, and I shepherd the children inside to begin again the endless task of cleaning up.

We sweep and scrub and clean the dust inside the house as best we can, and Henry buries the sheep in trenches made with the tractor and plough, and talks to the manager of Ulonga about repairing the fences. Then we write to Henry's middle brother, who is a lawyer. He writes to the Rural Reconstruction Board on our behalf, and after a long anxious wait, they agree to loan us enough to restock the property and mend the fences and the windmills to get the place running again.

And I am pregnant again. I am forty-four going on forty-five, too old to go through this again. But I must.

Anna is born in February 1940. My swan song.

No exit

As I sit in the wicker chair in the kitchen nursing Anna, I feel trapped with this small dependent being, so much work waiting to be done, and no prospect of rain. It is the driest year since we've been here, and Henry is hand-feeding the small flock that is left. He won't restock until the season turns. It's no use, he says; we'd only lose them again. He sold off all young ewes and wethers that were saleable when the winter rains failed to come. The river has shrunk to a string of shallow pools between islands of sand and mud and the water in the house tank is down to less than a quarter.

The mood is dark, with brooding storm clouds massing in the March skies every afternoon, promising rain but remaining closed, except at the end of the day when the sun has sunk. Then alluring shafts of blue-white sheet lightning dazzle the house and the bend and fireworks erupt on the horizon in spectacular chains, zigzags and forks of alien light. The strange beauty thrills me and, forgetting my cares, I rejoice in being here at the end of the world with no exit.

In the evenings, Henry watches for fires struck by lightning in dry grass on the treeless plains. He has drums of water set up on the back of the truck, and bags and spades loaded. He gets the boys to watch with him, playing a game of spot the smoke. He rides the pony up and down the driveway where it swings east, while they perch up in the gum trees at the front of the garden, seeing who can throw gumnuts the furthest. There are a few cries of 'Smoke, Dad, smoke!' but nothing close enough to home to worry about.

There is no relief from the heat. The only things that seem to thrive are the flies buzzing around the Coolgardie safe, where the last of the salted meat from an ageing ewe Henry killed last week is wrapped in a damp tea towel behind the gauze.

Even the ants are stirred up. They form long columns outside the kitchen and war with each other till slaughtered bodies lie in little heaps. Perhaps it is their way of keeping the population down. We are at war too, far away in the Pacific and in Europe, and every day the news brings more reports of casualties, of Hitler's ruthless drive to conquer Europe.

We don't have much to say to each other these days. When he's done the outside chores in a desultory way, he harnesses the horse and pulls the sulky out of the shed. The Chev broke down last week, and he hasn't ordered the parts to fix it yet.

'Come with me, Martha. A break will do us good. Give the little ones an outing too.'

'No, Henry, I'll stay. You go if you must. My feet are sore, and I have to make sure Malcolm does his schoolwork. And Anna's still taking a lot of time to feed. And Simon has to be kept on a tight rein, otherwise he'll run wild.'

'Well, I have to talk to someone. I'll go mad if I stay here day in day out.'

Am I not someone?

*

We've put David and Vera in hostels at Hay so they can go to school; Vera will be starting high school next year, and David is a gifted student who needs a good grounding so he can get a scholarship and go to university.

Malcolm is five and starting his correspondence lessons, and Simon, an active three-year-old, is always getting into trouble. I don't have much stamina; the late pregnancy took its toll and my feet are crippled with rheumatism. My toe joints are swollen, and I have a painful bunion on each foot. I can't wear shoes, only broken down old slippers. So I won't go into town, though I have to once to see the doctor. He says I have a severe vitamin B deficiency from the pregnancy and a poor diet. He tells me I must eat wholemeal bread and have full-cream milk and fresh green vegetables. My breast milk supply has failed, and I have to mix Sunshine dried milk and bottle-feed Anna. When we can get bananas, I feed her mashed banana, and I make oatmeal porridge for her ever day.

I am too old for this.

While I do my work, I reflect on our situation. I am in this for better or worse, I know. Henry and I vowed to make a life here and raise a family. Sometimes I dream of Wollongong, of Father and Mother, of a life far from this place. But I can't go back. In any case, my ties with Wollongong are weak now that Father and Mother are gone.

At last, with my urging, Henry fixes the irrigation pump and sews some wheat and barley in the home paddock and lucerne behind the hen shed and we get a milking cow with a bit of money Irene sent. So by the time Anna is a year old, I am grinding our wheat and baking our own bread and we have fresh milk and cream, and Henry gets me a churn so I can make butter.

We still get dust storms sometimes. At least they've brought some good: seeds of perennial saltbush from South Australia. It is a small creeping tough plant that survives the harshest summer, and the sheep love it. It binds the soil together too. Some early summer rains have fallen and there's new grass veiling the paddocks with green, and we've restocked. We hope that the sheep will grow fine strong wool, and that the meat of the two-tooth wethers will be sweet, with a salty under-flavour from the saltbush.

But although there's promise that the hard times are passing, Henry is restless. Rather than buckling down and doing the tasks that he's put off for so long, he seeks the company of others and yarns the hours away with any swaggie or visitor who comes.

I've finished my work and Anna is napping in the cot on the veranda. I stretch out in my swinging canvas chair – a treat Henry got for me when I was pregnant this time – and close my eyes. Henry's been out at the woodheap for the past hour or so, yarning to a swaggie who turned up at lunchtime.

He comes in carrying his hat. 'Martha, I'm going to Wyalgie to get some petrol for the Chev. I've got it going again, but we haven't got enough juice to get to town in it.'

'Why don't you go to Ulonga? It's closer.'

'Well, I want to talk to the boss about borrowing their stump jump plough. There's a lot of old tree roots at the river end of the home paddock. I need to get them out so I can plant more barley and oats.'

'Oh. But I thought you were going to clear out the channel to the barley crop. It's not letting enough water through, and the crop is dying.'

'I know. Strewth, woman, I know what needs to be done and when. I do the outside work. I'll clear the channel soon.'

'Oh, Henry, you're always postponing urgent jobs and finding reasons for not doing them.'

'Get off my back! You'd drive a teetotaller to drink,' he shouts, his face red, blue eyes flashing.

'Henry, be quiet! You'll wake Anna. And I don't think you need much driving.'

'I'll see you later.' He turns and strides towards the screen door.

'When will you be back?'

'Sundown.' He throws the door open and bangs it behind him.

Anna wakes up with a start and cries. I sigh, and swing my feet to the ground. My rest is over.

Evening comes. The boys have fed the dogs and put the chooks in their yard.

Malcolm and Simon run in with some eggs, and Malcolm says, 'Mum, there's a hole in the fence. Dad'll have to fix it or the foxes'll get in and kill the chooks!'

'Hmmph. I'm not sure when your father will be home. I'll see what I can do.' I pick Anna up and get some pliers and a bit of wire from the shed, and Malcolm and Simon show me where the hole is.

The sun has slid behind the trees in the bend, and the galahs are squawking and jostling each other in the sugar gums. The chooks are on their perches, fluffing up their feathers and making little clucking noises.

I cobble up the hole as best I can, pick Anna up from the gravelled path where she is scooping pebbles into little mounds, and we head back to the house.

Three hours later, when the children are asleep and I am getting ready for bed, I hear the horse's hooves. I close my bedroom door and go to bed. There is no point saying anything to him. He's probably been drinking. He'd rant and rave and call me a nag, and worse. I've heard it all before.

My war

World War II rages on, and the papers carry long lists of men dead, wounded and missing in action. After the Japanese bomb the US Pacific fleet at Pearl Harbour, America is forced into the war. The Japanese are advancing in the Pacific nations, which fall like dominoes – the Philippines, Thailand, Malaya, Burma, Dutch East Indies, New Guinea, the Solomon Islands and Singapore, where fifteen thousand Australian soldiers are taken prisoner of war. Bali and Timor fall too, and closer to home Darwin is bombed. Many fear this is the start of a Japanese invasion of the Australian mainland.

Here we are, cut off from the urgent questions of life and death and freedom and preserving a way of life against the enemy. We talk about whether Henry should sign up. But his age is against him, and farmers are exempted from service. We still haven't recovered from the savage drought and dust storms and we have five children to raise, feed, clothe and educate. How can I do this all on my own and look after the place as well?

The closest the war comes to us is a large internment camp on the outskirts of Hay that houses 2,500 German and Austrian men. They came out on the transport ship *Dunera*, and are known as the *Dunera* boys. Some of them, I've heard, are musicians, artists, scientists, inventors. Regardless of whether they fled Germany to escape the persecution of the Jews, they are lumped together as enemy aliens and treated as less than human. I hate to think what it must be like for these educated men from a civilisation far older than this to be rounded up, separated from their families, deported as prisoners in an overcrowded ship and then herded into a concentration camp in the middle of what must seem to them a desert, hot, arid, flat and lifeless.

In 1943, they are moved to Victoria and replaced by Italian and Japanese prisoners of war and civilian internees. Some of these are Japanese merchant seamen who were part of the pearl fishing industry and are already elderly. Some die in the camp. Some are children of Japanese pearlers and have never been to Japan.

On the station to our west, adjoining our river paddock, there is an outpost camp for Italian prisoners of war. These are men of peasant stock who have been rounded up because of their nationality but are not considered a threat for any other reason. They are employed on the station and live in tents near the river bend. They come over sometimes to borrow the use of Henry's cross-cut saw, which they call 'pulla-me-come-pusha-me-go'.

They are friendly, happy souls, and love nothing better than to sit on a log and chat with Henry, smoking cigarettes rolled with tobacco he gives them. I make a big billy of tea and take it out to them with scones or cake from the morning's baking. They love the children. They make catapults for Simon and Malcolm and carve pieces of dry wood into boats to sail on the edge of the river. They exclaim over little Anna's golden curls and green eyes, give her piggyback rides and bring her wildflowers in the springtime. In the autumn they bring me mushrooms from the river flats and occasionally a perch or a Murray cod they've caught. Many of them, they tell me in broken English, have little ones of their own growing up without their fathers. They sigh and sometimes weep and hope the war will end soon so they can go back to their families.

My war is a daily one with my work, my worries, and keeping the children at their schoolwork. At least David and Vera are doing well at school and David is finishing up soon. He is my golden boy. I know he will rise above these rough beginnings. Grown out of the spots and the spare tyres of adolescence, he is confident, tall, handsome and intelligent. I want him to do Arts Law and be a city lawyer – no country town for him. For him alone, it has all been worthwhile.

Vera is set on being an actress, and wants to go to London to study at the Royal Academy of Dramatic Art. She is determined to go and says she will go to Sydney and get work as a waitress and save up for her trip to England. As for the RADA fees, she says she will win a scholarship. I worry about her choosing such a path. I think women are wives and mothers first, teachers or nurses second, or if they are less fortunate in family and education, secretaries, clerks, shop assistants, housemaids and factory workers.

Oh, I admit I wanted a man's life – to be a lawyer or a journalist – but having had children, I see that this is the most important job a woman has, to bring up her children to be good citizens, happy, respectable, well educated, successful, to make the world a better place. To act on a stage, to draw attention to oneself, doesn't fit my idea of womanhood and the values I've been brought up with.

But I can see that Vera is different. She is creative and artistic and dreams of the stage. She has a gift for languages too, like Irene, and a fine ear for music and poetry. And she is beautiful, my first girl. More beautiful than I ever was. Five inches taller than me already, longer in the body, with an erect carriage (like mine), thick, glossy, wavy golden-brown hair, large hazel eyes and fine features. But I insist that she stay at school until she has her leaving certificate. I want her to have a good education to fall back on, as I can't imagine her earning a decent living from acting. Nor is she likely to meet a man in the acting profession who can give her a gentlewoman's lifestyle.

*

It's a lovely autumn day in 1945, and I am at the kitchen bench cutting up peaches and apricots. Anna is helping me and Simon and Malcolm are out chopping wood. Preserving the fruit crop is a two-day labour – halving and destoning the fruit which the children have picked, cutting out the bird pecks, and then getting the children, with their little hands, to pack them cut side down in the jars. As the layers stack up, I pour the syrup over them, filling the jar to within an inch of the top. Then I put the rubber ring on the jar neck, fit on the metal lid and secure it with a clip. I pack the jars into the boiler and fill it with cold water, then set it on the stove till the water is just below boiling point. Then I move the pan to the back of the stove to keep it at that temperature for an hour. This wonderful system was invented by an English migrant, Joseph Fowler, who was astounded by the abundance of stone and citrus fruit in Australia. By the Depression years, Fowler had become a household name.

My solution to wartime rationing is to make each person in the family save their teaspoonful of sugar a day and put it in a jar, and by the time the bottling season comes I have enough to make the syrup.

Anna is on the high stool putting the last layer of peaches in the last jar when the music program on the ABC is interrupted with an announcement. I rush into the living room and turn the wireless up loud. Winston Churchill's voice rings out, declaring that on this day Germany has unconditionally surrendered. Having thanked Britain's splendid allies, he ends on a sombre note:

> We may allow ourselves a brief period of rejoicing; but let us not forget for a moment the toil and efforts that lie ahead. Japan, with all her treachery and greed, remains unsubdued. The injury she has inflicted on Great Britain, the United States, and other countries, and her detestable cruelties, call for justice and retribution. We must now devote all our strength and resources to the completion of our task, both at home and abroad. Advance, Britannia! Long live the cause of freedom! God save the king!

I dance back into the kitchen, pick Anna up and spin round and round with her, shouting, 'We've won! We've won!'

Malcolm and Simon come running in from the woodheap and I put Anna down and hold them all three in my arms.

When Henry comes home from the paddocks, I rush out to tell him and we hug and kiss. Henry goes to the home paddock where he keeps the mob for killing and catches a wether, and we have fresh meat for dinner, a change from the usual salted fare. We feast on best end neck cutlets crumbed and fried in butter, fresh field mushrooms grilled with a dob of butter on top of the stove, and early cauliflowers, Henry's pride and joy, small snowy white heads done in a cheese sauce.

Next day, I'm washing up the pots from the morning baking when Anna appears wearing her blue cotton dress and sandals, holding a hair brush and a pair of white ribbons. I dry my hands, sit down in the wicker chair and pull the small plump body against my knees. I brush the tangles out of her fine brown hair and tie it back on each side with a ribbon.

'Do you remember when you cut your plait off?'

'Yes, I hated it!'

She was about four years old when she took my sharp dressmaking scissors from my work basket on the veranda and ran out to the orchard. The first I knew of it was when she came into the kitchen. She stood in front of me with one plait hacked off and the scissors in her hands, head hanging.

'Anna, you naughty girl! What have you done to your beautiful hair! It's never been cut since you were born. Oh, it will never grow so long again, I'm sure.'

Tears rolled down her cheeks, and I called Vera, who was home for the holidays, practising her elocution in the bedroom she shares with me when she's home.

'Vera! Come and see what your little sister has done! Quickly!'

Vera laughed when she saw Anna's lopsided head. She wears plaits at school and when she is home she ties it up with rags to curl it more and brushes the thick golden-brown tresses with a hundred strokes night and morning.

'Oh, how can you laugh?. Her hair was long enough to sit on.'

'Well, it can't be helped. Anna, you're a silly little girl. Give me the scissors and I'll cut the other half off.'

When Vera finished, Anna's hair stood out like a mop around her head, a bush that had been shorn of all its long branches, neatly trimmed, but unnatural. Since then, her hair hasn't grown past shoulder length.

I watch her growing out of her chubby infancy, and wonder what sort of life she will have. Will we be able to give her a good education? Will she grow up to be a farmer's wife, like me, or will she find another destiny? My last child, my second daughter, and I have such hopes for her. Her life is unknown to me. I wish I could see into the future.

Summer 1946

I stand at the kitchen sink, washing the cooking pots after the early morning session of baking. In the height of summer, I always get up at dawn to do as much work as I can before the heat comes in. I pause to wipe sweat from round my eyes. The kitchen is probably ten degrees hotter than the rest of the house; I've had the fire stoked up to bake bread and scones. I try to do the day's baking before the sun hits the house, but I still have to keep the fire going for the necessary pots of tea and, in the afternoon, to cook the evening meal.

The early sunlight is bright white already, glancing off the dark shiny leaves of the mandarine and lemon trees. The baby galahs are rasping for food in the tall sugar gums at the top of the garden, and down in the bend, a couple of kookaburras are splitting their sides. I hated the galahs when I first came here, the alien wail of the babies clamouring for food and water all through the long hot summer days. But after a while, it became a background theme, a reassuring refrain as I work or rest on hot afternoons, and I began to watch for the colourful flock flying in formation above the trees in the evenings, wheeling and scudding through the evening sky, coming in to land on the branches, squabbling and jostling, gradually quietening, ruffling their feathers and tucking in for the night.

Life for them is simple. Would that ours was so predictable, so limited, that I didn't have to worry about how to pay the bills, how to feed the children, how to keep the place going, how to keep Henry working for our future through the bad seasons as well as the good.

Can I leave? Should I? So many times, I've imagined it – packing up a few things for myself and Anna when Henry is out in the paddocks. Then, when he goes off to the neighbours, walking the mile and a half up to the main road and waiting till someone comes along, flagging them down and begging a lift into town. Going to the hostel where Simon and Malcolm are boarding, getting them to pack their things, and catching the noisy smelly little motor train from Hay to Narrandera. A night at the Railway Hotel, lying awake, thinking of all we've left, listening to the rumble of the freight trains passing, the water glass rattling against the jug on the bedside table.

Next day, tumbling the children with me into the South-west Mail, and off to Sydney, sitting up all night, listening to the conductor call out the station names – Junee, Old Junee, Tocumwal, Coolamon, Grong Grong, Cootamundra, Harden, Yass, Goulburn – on, on through the tablelands, dozing now, listening to the children's soft breathing, as they lie curled up on the seat beside me.

Early morning through the smoke-grey outer suburbs of Sydney, the inner-city rows of terraces with jagged roofs, waking the children as the train shuffles along the meshed lines leading to Central station. All tumbling out at last, smelling of soot and sleep, finding a porter; then another train to Wollongong, where Irene meets us and drives us in her little green Singer to the old wooden house where I was born.

And then rebuilding our life, finding a teaching job, a place where we can live, where the children can have a good education, where drought and the Depression are bad memories, where I can have some control over my life and the children's.

Ah, but it's too hard.

As I sweep the rough concrete floor, I remember a story Henry's father told me about a woman in the Booligal district from a well-to-do Sydney family, who decided she'd had enough of the hard life and her violent, drunken husband. Bloody Waugh, they called him, and his brother was Civil Waugh.

She packed some things for herself and her children into a dress basket, walked to the front gate of the property, and waited till someone stopped and gave them a lift. This was in the days when there was only horse or foot power on the roads, and the railway line had just opened to passenger traffic. So much easier now, but still so hard.

A woman who leaves her husband, no matter the provocation, is a misfit in society, without the authority of marriage – an in-between, nobody, not a virgin, not a wife, not a widow, not a spinster – spoiled goods, ready game for the woman hunter who wants sex without obligation. What's more, she has no means of support, and must work at whatever she can to feed her children and keep them clothed.

Still worse is to be a woman whose husband leaves her. A man is a man, and it is expected that a good percentage of them will stray in middle age. But a woman who can't hold onto her man must be lacking something, and the inference people make is that she has failed to satisfy him, to fulfil her wifely duties. In terms of the law and society's mores, the man has status, no matter his misdeeds, whereas a woman, if she steps out of the frame chosen for her, is judged to have failed in her purpose in life.

Still, it might be the lesser of two evils, to pre-empt what is starting to seem inevitable, take the cards into my own hands, pack up and leave.

It seemed so right when I accepted Henry's proposal, and I had such dreams of our life together. Now, nearly twenty years later, I have no dreams left except the desperate one of escape, and the hard-to-kill hope that things might change. If I do leave, will Henry come after me, try to bring me back? I doubt it. He's lost interest in the place, in me, in his family, in trying to make a living from this unforgiving land, and spends most of his days off at the neighbours. He usually does a token round of the paddocks in the morning, checking the windmills and the fences, then he disappears for the rest of the day. He can escape without leaving.

But I still hope for change. A few good seasons would turn things round; the sheep would grow fat on the spring grasses, the wool on the sheep would grow long and finely crimped and fetch a good price; the ewes would breed a fine flock of healthy lambs, girls to raise as breeding ewes, and boys to become wethers and be sold for the table. We might even be able to pay off our big debt to the Rural Reconstruction Board and make a few improvements to the house and the outside arrangements. Perhaps get a decent vehicle to replace the old Chev, which can't be relied on to get us into town. And plan for the children's future education.

Anna appears, still in pyjamas, her fine brown hair snarled by sleep.

'Good morning, darling,' I say. 'Go and get dressed, and make your bed. And don't forget to empty the pot!'

Although I didn't want to have any more babies, I cherish this last one, who grew into a chubby toddler with a floss of golden curly hair. She is still plump, but her hair has turned brown and lost its baby curls. She is the last fruit of our love. I married a man my opposite in so many ways – feisty, ardent, gregarious, gay and affectionate at his best, clever with his hands; at his worst, argumentative, hot-tempered and impatient, quick to tire of a hard task. A flash in the pan – look at all the things he has tried and abandoned, the machinery that has broken down and not been repaired – the generator, which briefly gave us electric light, the irrigation pump, the tractor, the Chev.

I caught fire from his passion for life on the land, burned slowly and am still smouldering. He flared up in a bright flame and was soon spent. I wonder how much longer he will last here.

My mother stopped writing in her diary for years after this. I have none of her words for what she was going through, only the few things she said to me about her worries at the time, and I can only imagine how her desire to stay on the place she loved fought with her bitterness, her disappointment, her yearning to escape the heartbreaking struggle that her marriage had become.

My early childhood was happy, and I had little awareness of the deep fractures in my parents' relationship until it broke apart. I saw our world quite differently from how she saw it, yet, as I came to realise, we shared a deep bond with the place. I did not see the failures and mistakes my father made, and the harsh facts of climate and the struggle to sustain our life did not weigh on me. They were simply an external part of the world as I knew it, and I created my own magic spaces within it.

Then everything changed.

Anna's Story

A little world, July 1946

The grass is hazed with white and crackles when I step on it. I turn the tap on to wash out the chamber pot but no water comes out. The birds aren't making much noise; just a few sparrows are chirping. They're snuggled in their nests till the sun comes up and warms the air. The middle of the sky is dark blue and the edges are pale pink and there's a rosy glow above the trees in the bend. The water in the irrigation ditches is iced over and if you step on it, your foot will crack through the ice and sink into the deep cold mud. When spring comes, the ice will melt and the frogs will lay their eggs and tadpoles will hatch and thick green grass will grow along the banks. Wildflowers will pop up among the grass, bachelor's buttons like little creamy pincushions, pink and purple vetches with tiny flowers shaped like the sweet peas in Dad's garden, star-shaped purple flowers I don't know the name of and buttercups that shine a golden light on your face if you hold them under your chin.

I leave the pot on the grass and run inside.

Mum stands at the big green sink washing the dishes in soapy water. 'Here's your porridge, Anna. Sit down by the stove and eat it and then you can have some toast and honey.'

The logs in the firebox hiss and sputter, and my chilblains are burning. I take my empty plate and bowl to Mum and climb on a fruit box so I can reach the top of the bench. Mum's got a little wire cage on a handle she keeps a cake of yellow soap in – Sunlight, it's called – and shakes it in the hot water to make suds that clean the plates and things. She hands each dish to me and I dip it in a bowl of rinsing water then dry it. While she's scrubbing the pots, I put the crockery away in the cupboard. Then I take the cutlery to the dresser in the dining room. I put more logs on the fire from the pile on the hearth. Mum cleans out the ashes and whitewashes the bricks in the morning, then sets the fire and lights it before the rest of us get up. In winter, she lights the fire in the fireplace at the other end of the long room as well at night and lights the lamps, and after dinner we sit round the fire and talk and play cards and read.

I love this long room. We've got a couple of old brown armchairs covered in velvet. They're worn out and when you sit down, lumps of stuffing stick into your bottom. No one plays the piano but it's beautiful, shiny dark red and brown. When you look at it, you can see your face. The keys are yellow and some of the wood is peeling off. It came from the house where Dad lived when he was a little boy. On top of it there's a Chinese vase with a round belly and a narrow neck. It is pale pink like the edges of the sky when the sun sets. There are men painted on it. They wear strange clothes, pants with legs that are puffy above the knee and tight below, and jackets with long billowy sleeves, crimson inside and gold, black and red on the outside. What are the men doing, why do they wear such rich clothes, and where are the women and children?

The floorboards are bare and most of the dark colour has worn off. Mum sweeps the floor every day and mops it a couple of times a week, and sometimes she daubs polish over it then ties some rags to our shoes so we can scoot up and down and make it shine.

'Anna! While you're in there, sweep up the crumbs on the floor round the table and the ash round the fireplace, please. Then you can do the kitchen floor while I make a cake and some scones for the men's smoko.'

I hate sweeping the kitchen floor. It's rough and most of the dirt doesn't come off.

I'm Cinderella and Mum's the wicked stepmother who makes me do all the hard work. Oh, fairy godmother come and help me find my prince! She appears in a shower of stars and waves her wand. My old skirt and jumper turn into a ball gown of white organdie embroidered with rosebuds. There are layers and layers of frothy lace petticoats underneath and a soft feather wrap around my neck. The straw broom becomes the coachman wearing gold livery and a white curly wig. He leads me to the gate, where the old sulky has changed into a shiny brown coach with red velvet seats and curtains. Bess the old bay mare is a prancing white steed wearing a gold bridle and harness studded with red and blue and green and yellow jewels that sparkle brighter than the stars.

'Don't stand there dreaming, Anna!' Mum says, dropping the wooden spoon she's beating the cake with. 'You've left half the dirt behind. Here, give me the broom. I'll give it a thorough sweep later.' She takes it and stands it in the corner near the stove. 'Just get the dustpan and sweep up the dust. Then get your book. I haven't time to correct your lessons while the shearing's on, so you can use the time to read.'

I do correspondence lessons. They come from Sydney in a big brown envelope once a fortnight and when I've finished all the work, Mum sends them back. Simon and Malcolm do them too but Mum says they'll go to school in Hay next year and stay at the hostel like Vera and David. David wants to be a lawyer and Vera wants to go to London to be an actress.

Last night when I went to bed, I heard Mum and Dad arguing.

'The boys can only go to school if we get a good price for the wool clip,' Dad said in an angry voice.

'Henry, just because you didn't finish your secondary education doesn't mean they shouldn't. They deserve to have a good education.'

'Just because you got a fancy degree doesn't mean your kids have to.'

'It's not about me or you, it's about our kids and what they need to set them up in life, to get a degree and a profession. It's worth a sacrifice.'

'Sacrifice be buggered! We might not even be able to feed ourselves! You're not living in the bloody city now. This is the outback!' he shouted.

Footsteps, a door slamming. Mum sighed and the fire crackled. She must have poked it to boil the kettle again.

I'm not going to university when I'm big! I sweep the dust into the dustpan. I want to stay here forever. I'm going to be a farmer's wife. I'll marry someone handsome and kind and funny like Dad and we'll live by the river. We won't be poor, we'll own a lot of land with a big homestead and a cook and someone to do the cleaning. There'll be a tennis court and a boat and horses and we'll have parties people come to from miles around, and we'll go to Sydney for the Royal Show and win prizes for our wool.

*

The warm air in the kitchen smells of smoke and gum leaves. I get my book and snuggle into the wicker chair. *New Fairy Tales* has no colour pictures, just a few little drawings at the beginning of each story. I know most of the stories by heart.

Kay and Gerda are playing among the roses in their window box garden when a splinter of the troll mirror pierces Kay's eye and enters his heart. I know what will happen next. He gets cross and nasty and teases Gerda all the time instead of playing with her. Like Simon and Malcolm do sometimes.

David is my favourite in the family after Dad, but he's away most of the time. When he comes home, he plays with me sometimes and reads me stories. Last time he was home, he read me *Alice in Wonderland*. I love how Alice falls down the rabbit hole and goes through a magic door and meets all those crazy people and animals. I wanted to keep sitting on his knee and listening to her adventures. I was sad when he shut the book and said, 'And that's the end of the book, Pook!'

One day, Kay hitches his sled to the Snow Queen's sleigh and follows her to the North Pole and Gerda sets off to find him in the land of ice and snow. I've never seen snow. If the plains were all covered with snow and the sun stayed under the earth, it would be like the North Pole and Bess would be a reindeer and the sulky a sled and I'd set out to find Kay and rescue him from the wicked Queen. And we'd live happily ever after.

Summertime

On late summer nights after days of scorching heat, electrical storms rage. Lightning flashes in sheets and trees and paddocks shine with a weird light. Sometimes the black sky splits open with jagged edges of forked light. After dinner we sit in the lamplight. The cedar tree on the front lawn lights up. I climb onto Dad's knee and slide my hand around his neck.

'Sheet lightning's harmless,' he says. 'But not the chain and fork kinds. They can start fires in the dry grass. They can kill you.'

'Do they kill sheep too?' I ask.

'You bet. Sheep, cattle, anything, even trees. But the most deadly is ball lightning. It drifts through the air, and it'll kill you instantly if it touches you.'

'Have you ever seen ball lightning?' Malcolm asks.

'Yep. Saw it kill a man out Booligal way. We were camping out mustering sheep on Dad's place near the Lachlan. We were riding back from a muster late one afternoon in March. Bloody great ball of blue fire just drifted through the trees and hit the chap in front of me. He fell off his horse stone dead.'

'Henry,' Mum says, 'don't scare them! We've never seen ball lightning here on the Murrumbidgee. And don't swear, please.' Her face shines yellowy-white in the lamplight and she makes a clicking noise with her tongue like she always does when she is cross. She stands up and starts clearing the table. 'Come on, children. Let's get the washing up done and then it's your bedtime.'

When we go to bed on the front veranda, where we sleep in the summertime, we pull back the stripy canvas blinds, poke our heads under them and watch for the next flash or shaft. We count seconds until the thunderclap that follows – a second for each mile – to see how far away the storm is and guess where lightning might strike. Mostly we can count up to ten or more, for the big storms happen on the open plains. The storm moves away after a while and stars glimmer among the clouds. We let the blinds drop down again.

There are many holes in the blinds, magic eyes we use to see, name and count the stars as they appear in the night sky. We kneel on Malcolm's bed, eyes pressed against the jagged holes. The stars are a milky scarf thrown over the dark shoulders and breasts of the sky.

*

One summer day it's so hot I can hardly breathe. Mum says the thermometer shows it's one hundred and twenty degrees Fahrenheit. No one does any work. We put our bathers on and go down to the sandy beach in the bend, where a tall river gum shades the water. Its trunk is smooth and white and its grey-green pointy leaves droop down into the green water. The water seems almost still with tiny ripples here and there around a twig or a snag, then it slides more quickly round a curve in the bank. The edges are shallow and you can see the sandy bottom. There is a big snag you can hang onto or climb on and jump into the deeper water. Down there in the deep cool green part where you can't see, big fish swim.

Mum wears an old loose dress tucked up above the knees and sits near the edge with the water lapping over her legs and feet. She says she doesn't have any bathers and can't swim. I can only dog paddle but I'm not afraid of the water; it's soft and cool and flows so slowly at our swimming spot. In winter when it rains heavily, it flows much faster and then I'm scared of it.

I splash on the sandy bank and paddle out to the snag. The boys race each other out to a sandy island and back. Dad floats on his back in the shade of the big tree. His face is spotted with leaf shadows and his eyes are shut. His hair floats like river reeds. Mum calls us in and hands out biscuits and cups of ginger beer. Dad rolls a cigarette and lies back on the sand with his head resting on a rolled-up towel.

Mum sits beside him doing the crossword in the newspaper. She reads the clues. 'Leafy shelter?'

'Arbor?' He says and blows some smoke rings.

'Yes, that's good. Short thick sticks used for fighting?'

'Dunno.' He stubs his cigarette out in the sand and rolls over onto his tummy to have a snooze. His hair flops over his forehead.

I take the tyre tube into the river downstream from the boys and step into it. I float through the rippling light and shadow into the trees and deep sky.

There's only the sound of the river singing and the cicadas clickety-clicking like a thousand pairs of knitting needles.

Dad

Dad's really good with animals. He's given me a poddy lamb to look after. His mum wouldn't feed him, so Dad brought him home, and we called him Curly.

'It's your job to feed him, Holly.' He gives me a bottle filled with Sunshine milk, and shows me how to hold it.

Curly's only little, but he's really strong, and I have to sit down with my back to a post or a tree while he sucks and butts against the bottle and wiggles his tail. He follows me everywhere, and soon he's big enough for me to walk with my arm round his neck. When I go inside, he bleats and hangs around the back door until I come out again. I'd like to let him inside, but Mum says no.

Dad's favourite horse is a pony called Nicky. He is short and fat, a bright orangey-brown colour. He doesn't like being caught and saddled. You have to trick him with a bunch of juicy thistles or cabbage leaves. When you do up the girth, he puffs out his stomach so you have to put the spike in a hole further out. Then when you climb on, he lets his breath out so the saddle is loose. I'm not allowed to ride him unless someone holds the reins and leads him. Sometimes he gets frisky and kicks up his hind legs, and once when Malcolm was on him he reared up so he was standing up on two legs. Malcolm fell off and got a big bump and a cut on his head. Mum had to bathe it and bind it up with strips of white sheet cut up.

'His mother is a circus pony,' Dad says. 'That's where he learned his tricks. He's a clever one! Watch this.'

He feeds him the makings of a cigarette, first the tobacco then the paper and last the match. Nicky munches it all up and looks for more.

'Watch for the smoke!' Dad laughs.

Mum tells us that Nicky is the father of several foals and fillies. One was The Creamy. She broke a leg and Dad made her better. The jackeroos from Ulonga said he should shoot her, that she'd never be any good as a saddle horse again. But Dad rigged up a frame under the gum trees to take the weight off her leg and put her in it. He kept her there and fed and watered her until the leg was better, and then he took her out and let her roam free until she got her strength back, then he rode her again.

'She was as good as new!' Mum said. 'He has a way with animals, your father. When I first came here, he had several animals that had been with him from the beginning. They followed him when he was working near the house. There they'd go in a line wherever he went, two dogs, a cat, a pet lamb and a rooster.'

Sometimes when Dad's finished his work, we walk in the garden, just the two of us, his arm around me. I love him so much, I want to marry him when I grow up. I want to live with him always.

Sometimes we shout and chase each other and he lets me catch him and we roll over and over down the grassy orchard slope while the Rhode Island Red hens scatter squawking and spreading their clipped wings.

At night when he's finished his work and had a shower, Dad sits me on his knee and tells me stories about when he was a little boy, as we watch the flames curl around the glowing log.

'We had an Irish handyman called Patrick. He made me a cart I could sit or stand in, and he'd pull me along in it. He wrote the words "Royal Male" on the side of it.'

Mum walks past. 'Hmmph! He probably meant to put "Royal M-a-i-l".'

Dad ignores her and throws another log on the fire. The log spits and sap oozes out when the flames lick round it.

He holds a hand out, then passes it through the orange flame that shoots up. 'See? I'm magic. But don't you try it, you'll get burnt. When I was about your age, Holly, my dad taught me to ride a horse. He'd hold the rein and guide my horse along, riding ahead at a trot. When I got sick of bumping up and down, I'd tell him the mozzies were biting me, so he'd stop and take me on his horse.'

'Will you teach me to ride properly, Dad?' The boys can ride, but I'm not allowed to ride on my own.

'When you're a bit bigger, Holly.'

'How much bigger?'

Dad points to a mark on the door frame. 'See that? That was how tall Simon was when he learned to ride. Maybe next summer.'

He pulls an old book called *Farthest North* off the mantelpiece. It's tied together with string, so he puts me down while he unties it and turns the pages.

'See there? That's my grandfather's name. He was a wealthy merchant and when he died he left a lot of money to set up a home for "elderly retired gentlewomen of reduced circumstances" in Norway. And his name is in this book because he donated a lot of money to an expedition to the North Pole – the same amount as the King of Norway. The ship was specially built to withstand the pressure of the ice. When it got frozen into the ice, they hoped it would drift over the North Pole. But it didn't, so the captain decided to try and reach it on foot. He set out with his first mate; they took sleds and twenty-four dogs, but they couldn't reach the pole, because there were steep ridges in the ice all going the wrong way. They had to turn back and one by one they killed the dogs and ate them, except for the last one, who was their pet, but he got sick and they had to shoot him.'

I turn my head away. How horrible. Fancy eating their own dogs. Fancy having to shoot their pet dog. I've seen Dad kill a dog after it mauled a sheep. It wasn't our pet but it still made me feel sick to see him do it.

'Once a dog gets a taste of fresh blood,' he'd said as he put the rifle away, 'you can never trust it again.'

Dad goes on with the story. 'After that, they lived on whatever they could shoot – birds, sometimes a walrus or even a polar bear. When the ice they were walking on started to break up, they turned their sleds into kayaks. The first land they reached was a tiny rocky outcrop, and they called it after Grandfather. They went on to a bigger island that had grass and trees and some wildlife, and dug out a shelter there. When winter came, they stayed inside except when they had to catch food. Then in the spring they were rescued by an English explorer and his men, who took them back to the mainland. And by a miracle, the ship had got free of the ice and the men on it came home safely about the same time. They'd been frozen in for three years and no one died.'

He ties the book up again and puts it back on the mantelpiece. He heats a poker in the coals and burns pictures with it into a piece of wood he has sanded and rubbed smooth. The boys drop the Mechano they're building on the rug and come over and watch.

'I'll finish it tomorrow,' he says, yawning. He picks up his mouth organ and plays tunes until supper-time.

Mum brings a loaf of bread from the kitchen and cuts some thick slices. He toasts them on a long fork and cooks a pot of field mushrooms with cream and a knob of butter. It's yummy, but the yummiest supper he makes for special occasions is puftaloons, little scones fried in dripping and filled with golden syrup

After supper, he reads to us from one of our favourite books. Dad likes *The Specialist*, about a man who built outdoor dunnies in all shapes and sizes, from single-seaters to four- or six-seaters. Mum always says she couldn't use anything other than a single-seater, and Dad teases her and says he'll build us a seven-seater.

Another one we love is *The Songs of a Sentimental Bloke*. Dad likes to recite some of the Bloke's lines:

> I done me block complete on this Doreen,
> An' now me 'eart is broke, me life's a wreck!
> The dreams I dreamed, the dilly thorts I thunk
> Is up the pole, an' joy 'as done a bunk.
> Wimmin! O strike! I orter know the game!
> Their tricks is crook, their arts is all dead snide.

He stops and gazes at the glowing log, which collapses with a soft sigh.

'All right, children,' Mum yawns, 'it's bedtime.'

No place for a girl

Mum packs scones and sultana cake, a big Thermos of tea and pannikins into a basket and we set off for the sheep yards down near the bend.

The ewes and half-grown lambs are crowded into a big yard that has a narrow race leading to a gate that swings open into two separate yards. Dad and another man stand at the gate as Simon and Malcolm and the two dogs force the animals down the race. Bluey, the collie-kelpie cross, jumps up on the backs of the sheep, barking and dancing from one to another. Nugget, his mum, stays behind the sheep, urging them on by darting from one side to the other, nudging the tails or legs of any she can reach.

As the sheep come to the gate, the men swing it from side to side so the lambs have to go into one yard and the ewes into the other. When they've all gone through, the men move into the lamb yard, and the marker pulls a knife and another tool from a pouch on his belt. Dad grabs a lamb and holds it up on the top rail. The man punches a hole in the lamb's ear first, then cuts something from its bottom. He throws a lump of flesh on the ground, then slices off most of the lamb's long tail. He drops the lamb down and it runs off bleating and spattering blood on the ground. The man wipes the knife on a cloth while Dad grabs another lamb.

Flies swarm round the bloody bits near the men's feet. The lambs cry in high scared bleats and the ewes answer in deeper voices.

'Henry! Smoko's here,' Mum calls above the bleating and the dogs' barking.

He looks up and sees me standing behind Mum. He walks over to the fence and takes the basket then turns to me. 'Gedaway, girl! This is no place for ya!'

The man slides his knife and marking tool into the pouch and pulls a packet of tobacco from his pocket, then feels in his shirt pocket for matches and papers. The boys climb over the fence and sit in the shade of a tree, and Dad walks over to them and puts the basket down. The dogs squeeze under the fence and flop near them, panting and dripping saliva in the dirt.

The killing shed is below the shearers' hut at the edge of the bend. The sun has gone behind the trees and the sky is soft blue and pink at the edges. I wriggle into a fork between the branches of the big tree on the river bank. I think of Curly, his woolly crinkly neck that I wrap my arm around when he trots beside me, his soft velvety lower lip, the row of milk teeth that nibble my fingers. He has two bumps on his forehead where his horns will grow. Dad says he will be too big for me to play with soon and he'll have to be put out in the paddocks with the other sheep. I don't want him to go.

Dad's standing over a fat woolly sheep lying on its side. He puts his knee behind its shoulder and pulls its head back so its neck is arched. He pulls a knife with a sharp point from a sheath hanging from his belt, and stabs it into the neck near the ear, then cuts right across and snaps the head back. Blood spurts and makes a shiny dark pool on the ground. He sticks the knife in again and works it back and forwards. The sheep twitches and kicks its legs. He cuts the head right off and sets it on the bench. The dogs lean forward, licking their lips.

I climb down from the tree and scramble down the river bank. My stomach heaves and some burning green stuff spills out of my mouth and falls in a thin stream into the river. I bend down and splash my face and take a mouthful of sweet cool water.

Vera

It's nearly Christmas time and Vera is home on holiday. She spends a lot of time in Mum's bedroom, where she reads lots of silly rhymes out loud. Simon and Malcolm and I are outside the window weeding the flower bed.

'Box and Cox are two little men, Box weighs one pound and Cox weighs ten,' she chants.

We drop our hoes and prance up and down, softly repeating what she says, pursing our lips and trying to make the sounds come out rounded and clear like she does. I trip over the wheelbarrow and fall, and we burst into giggles.

Vera raises the window and sticks her head out, shaking her golden-brown, wavy hair at us. She's frowning and looks cross. 'Go away, you silly children! Go and weed somewhere else. I have to practise my elocution!'

Simon and Malcolm run round the corner. I stand still, silently mouthing Vera's rhyme, rounding my lips for the o's and nodding my head for emphasis. What would it be like to be an actor and stand on a stage in front of dozens of people, acting out someone else's life? Who could I pretend to be?

'Hey, Anna! There're some big fat grasshoppers in here! Betcha not game to eat one. They're yummy!'

I can hear Simon making sucking noises, like he's drinking hot tea out of a saucer. I walk slowly to the old broken rainwater tank near the tamarisk tree and climb in. There are lots of dead grasshoppers. They come in clouds sometimes, making the sky dark and eating everything green. There was an attack a week ago and there are still a few flying around.

Simon picks one up and tosses it into his mouth. 'Mmmm, dee-licious. Go on, try one.'

I look for a small one and stuff it into my mouth. If I swallow it quick I won't taste it.

'Yah! You have to chew it.' Simon says. 'See?' He opens his mouth and pokes out his slimy green tongue.

'Yuk! I feel sick.' I climb out of the tank and spit out the hairy horrible thing then run towards the dunny. I need to wee.

Vera is sitting on the hole, her skirts spread out, reading a magazine. 'Get out!' She frowns at me and turns the page over.

I stick my tongue out at her and sit outside with my back against the wall. She doesn't come out. I can't wait any longer. I let the wee out hot and tingly. It makes a big puddle around me.

'You dirty little girl!' Vera says as she walks past. 'Go and tell Mother you've wet your pants.' She gives me a disgusted look and walks off to the house.

*

'Hurry up, girl, for Chrissake! You're as slow as a bloody wet week!' Dad yells, pacing up and down in the living room.

Mum sits at the table with her best hat on, writing a shopping list. She's frowning, her mouth sucked in over her teeth in a straight line so you can't see her lips.

Vera opens the bedroom door and steps into the living room.

Dad lets out a slow whistle. 'Crikey! What a stunner.'

Vera's wearing a new dress she's made. It is seersucker cotton with little orange, red and yellow flowers on a chocolate-brown background. The neck is scooped, the sleeves puffed and the waist fits tight. The skirt is long, round her ankles, hanging in soft folds.

'It's the new look. Do you like it?' Vera spins around on her high-heeled white sandals and the skirt flares out showing her full frilly petticoat. Her long hair swings as she spins. Her hands resting on her hips are creamy white and her long nails are painted scarlet. She smiles in a slow sort of way showing the tips of her white teeth through shiny red lips.

We pile into the Chev. Vera and Mum and Dad sat in the front and the boys and I climb into the back tray and sit on the hessian bags.

On the main road a mile or two from the front gate, the engine starts to sputter and cough. Then it stops. The boys jump down and stand beside the bonnet.

Dad lifts the side flap up and peers in, pokes around a bit then slams it shut and gets the crank handle and tries to start it. He turns furiously. He straightens, takes a deep breath then cranks again. He throws the crank handle at the door. 'Curse ya! Ya bloody blasted useless heap of fuckin' junk!'

'Henry! Please! There's no need for such foul language. Anna, get down and bring a couple of hessian bags with you.' Mum's face is pinched tight against the glare as she looks up and reaches out her hands to take the bags from me.

Dad opens the bonnet again and reaches in. The boys watch and pass him tools while he grunts and curses.

Mum takes my hand and leads me away from the truck across the road to the fence. Vera follows, picking her way through the tussocky grass and prickle bushes that grow beside the road. We climb through the fence, taking it in turns to hold the wires apart and sit down under the tree to wait. Vera slips her sandals off. She rubs the dirt off the heels with an edge of the hessian bag and sets them neatly together beside her. She sighs and runs her hands over her legs, picking grass seeds one by one out of her nylon stockings. She folds her arms round her knees and tucks her head down, closing her eyes.

Mum takes her hat off and rests her head against the tree trunk. There is a red line on her forehead from the hat, and her hair is wet with sweat. Her eyes are open, staring across the bare paddocks.

Dad gets the truck going again, but it's sputtering and hiccuping, so we turn and head back home. Vera goes to Mum's bedroom to lie down with a headache – 'It's the heat! It was unbearable out there' – and Mum goes to lie in her swinging chair on the veranda. Dad is in a bad mood, and makes the boys help him pull the engine apart.

I find my favourite book, *Snugglepot and Cuddlepie*, and take it out to the apple tree. It's shady and cool here, and I can nestle in the hollow where the branches spread out from the main trunk. In spring and summer I come here when I want to be alone and no one knows where I am. In springtime the tree is covered in cream and pink blossoms and fresh green leaves. The apples aren't ripe yet, they're bright green with a blush of red and a downy coating that I rub off. I love the tart sharp taste. I eat lots, seeds and all, leaving only the stalk. I talk to the sparrows, wrens, willy wagtails, bees, white moths, caterpillars and flying insects. I tell them all my secrets. Out here in the apple tree I am queen of the orchard and no one can change anything unless I say so, nothing breaks, and no one gets cross.

*

David didn't come home for Christmas this year. He's living in the city, studying, and Mum says he has to work in the holidays to pay for his keep. I miss him. He sent us a card and some books. Mine is *Blinky Bill*, about a naughty koala who's always getting into trouble and having adventures.

Vera gives us a gramophone. When you open it, there is a round disc you put a black record on and a shiny arm that swings down with a needle on the end. Before you put the needle on the record, you have to wind a handle on the side. If you don't wind it up enough, the sound goes funny and the voices slow down and get deep and muffled. Part of the present is some records, Spike Jones singing 'Beetle Bomb', and two of Danny Kaye's. The boys like the one that plays 'Minnie the Moocher', but I like the story of 'Tubby the Tuba' and how he became the star of the band.

We all get a bit tipsy on Mum's hop beer. It isn't supposed to make you drunk, but sometimes it goes funny when it's fermenting. The bottles are stacked on the back veranda, and on hot days a cork might shoot out of the bottle with a noise like a gunshot, spraying beer all over the floor.

Mum doesn't look too pleased when we play the records over and over again, but Dad laughs every time we play 'Beetle Bomb'. He's a racehorse who ran last for most of the race and amazed everybody by passing all the other horses to come first.

Mum washes up and we dry the dishes. Malcolm piles the dinner plates up and carries them to the dresser. He trips on the rug and the plates fly out of his hands and smash on the floor.

Mum runs in from the sink, dish mop in her hand, her mouth hanging open. 'Oh, my lovely dinner set! It was a wedding present!' she wails.

Malcolm rushes out the kitchen door and Vera follows him. When I go out to the shed to find a box to put the broken bits in, he is sitting on a log near the wood heap. He is crying, and Vera has her arm around him.

I feel sorry for Malcolm too. He couldn't help it that the rug got in his way. He was trying to help Mum. He doesn't often get in trouble. It's usually Simon or me. Mum's often cross now, and scolds us for everything. Vera does what she likes, and David's away most of the time. I miss him. Vera doesn't like me much, I think she's jealous of me because I'm the littlest, but she really likes Malcolm and makes a fuss of him when she's at home.

Swede turnips

Turnips again on the dinner plate. We call them turnips, but Dad says their proper name is swede turnips. Maybe they're called swedes because the Swedes like eating them. I don't. I've eaten the stew, a chop with gravy, carrot and potato, and the cabbage. I flatten the turnip mound and make noughts and crosses on it with the edge of my knife.

Dad looks across at my plate. 'What about the starving people in India?' he yells. 'They'd be glad of whatcha turning yer nose up at and what's on yer plate'd keep a whole family alive for a week!'

I don't care. I'm not going to eat it. I sit and watch the others eat their pudding. Jam sponge and custard, one of my favourites. No one speaks to me. The others get up, clear the table around me and wash up.

Dad walks back into the room. 'You'll sit there till you eat that up, Anna. You don't know what's good for you.' His face is red and creased, his blue eyes flashing like knives.

Horrid man. I hate you. I hope you fall down a rabbit hole and break your leg.

I make roadways and hills in the yellow pasty muck. Simon and Malcolm snigger at me as they go off to bed. Simon pokes me in the back and makes a face as if he is choking, grabbing his throat and rolling his eyes to the ceiling.

'Gedout. I hate you. You'll be sorry.' I lift my fork and thrust it at him.

He pokes out his chest and screws up his face.

'Ugly, you're so ugly. The wind'll change!' I mutter.

'Simon!' Mum calls from the kitchen. 'Get to bed at once.'

Tomorrow when I'm making their beds I'll short-sheet them and put a roly-poly burr bush in Simon's. Then I'll write a note and stick it on his pillow with a rose thorn: 'I'll DO you!'

The fire is nearly out. The kerosene lamp is sputtering and the tablecloth is black with dead midges. Mum's gone to bed and Dad is on the front veranda smoking.

I could chuck the turnip muck in the back garden and pretend I've eaten it. But he'll probably find it in the morning and make me eat more.

The clock strikes nine. I open my mouth, squeeze my eyes shut and shovel it down.

Next morning, Dad goes out with the horse and sulky to collect the mail from the railway siding. He tells us to weed the paths and the melon bed while he's away. Malcolm and I are weeding the front path that goes from the kitchen garden to the gate, scraping the hoe along to get rid of the little creeping plants, but Simon is shirking.

'Eh! Come 'n' watch me chuck the old man's bloody old turnips in the river!' he yells from the shed.

We drop our hoes and run over to where he is standing.

'Gaahn. I betchya too scared,' Malcolm says.

'Just watch me.' He heaves the first bag of turnips up onto his shoulder, staggers over to the riverbank and tosses it into the swiftly flowing water.

'Hooray!' Malcolm shouts.

Simon turns around, his face pale, his eyes glassy, and runs back to get the next bag. He does this until all the turnips are gone.

Late in the afternoon, I'm in the dunny. The hornet is buzzing round its nest in the corner of the roof. It has a red-brown middle, a pointy orange bottom, and fuzzy golden hair round its head. Its legs and wings are toffee colour and its eyes and beaky nose are like polished stones. Does it have babies? How does it make them? I pull a square of newspaper from the hook on the wall. I wipe my bottom and drop the paper down the hole, then stand up and sprinkle borax on the pile.

'Simon, you little bugger! Wait till I catch you! Where're all my swedes gone?' Dad yells.

I pull my pants up and rush out. Simon is climbing the big silver gum near the dunny but Dad catches him before he can get high enough and pulls him down. He holds him with one hand and pushes him over. With his other hand, he undoes his belt and pulls it off. He stretches his arm back behind him then brings the belt forward with a jerk and whacks Simon across the buttocks. Whack whack whack whack whack whack. Simon's snot and tears dribble onto the ground, making a dirty puddle. Big red welts burst out of the white flesh of his bottom.

'Get inside and go to bed!' Dad yells. 'No dinner for you tonight! I'll make you eat bloody swedes every day! I'll get some more from Ulonga.'

I feel sorry for him. He's always getting in trouble with Dad, because he doesn't do as he's told and he answers back. He was just trying to save us from having to eat that horrible muck. When we eat dessert, I scrape a bit of jam roly-poly onto my bread and butter plate when Mum's in the kitchen and Dad's got his back turned, and I hide it behind the picture on the mantelpiece. After we've dried the dishes and put them away, I sneak it out to Simon in his bed.

He's lying curled up, facing the wall.

'Simon! I've brought you some pudding.'

He rolls over and pushes me away. 'Get lost!'

I stumble and fall plonk down on the next bed, but I don't drop the pudding. I think about eating it myself, but I'm not hungry. So I throw it outside for the ants to eat.

Next morning I'm in the back garden playing with Nobby the pup. Simon comes round the corner and pushes me over, then runs away. I scramble up and pick up a clod of dirt and throw it at his head. It misses. He turns, puffs out his chest and roars at me like a lion. I scream and throw myself at him. He grabs my arm and twists it behind my back.

Malcolm bursts out from the back veranda and runs over. He pushes Simon to the ground and falls on top of him. They roll in the dirt grunting and swearing. Malcolm punches Simon in the eye. Simon smashes his fist into Malcolm's nose and it starts to bleed.

I throw myself on top of them. 'Stoppit! Stoppit! Yer killing 'im!' I yell as I pound Simon's back.

He has Malcolm pinned down. He pushes his head back into the dirt, where the blood from Malcolm's nose is making a large puddle.

Nobby yelps, I scream for Mum and she charges out with a broom in her hand.

'Get up! You're a disgrace, the pair of you. Look at you! Get inside immediately – clean yourselves up.'

Boys are different

Since the boys started school in Hay, they're only home for holidays. So I play on my own, when I'm not doing my lessons or helping Mum. I make up imaginary creatures, fairies and princes and princesses. The fairies dance and sing and make the plants grow and the flowers bloom, and ride on the backs of the birds and the bees and butterflies, and weave magic spells and sometimes do mischievous things that the boys get blamed for. I'm usually a beautiful princess, but sometimes I get switched when I'm a baby and grow up with a poor woodcutter and his wife, until a prince finds me and sees a birthmark on my neck. He knows that the king and queen are looking for their lost daughter who has this mark, and he rescues me and takes me to the palace, and asks for my hand in marriage.

Sometimes I wish I had a real friend, someone to build cubbies with me and act out stories we make up.

When the boys are home, Malcolm is kind to me but when he's with Simon, they often go off and make up secret games I'm not allowed to join in. It's because I can spell now, and they can't spell out words to each other that they don't want me to understand like they used to.

I'm playing out on the riverbank near the old windmill, making a little house of grass and twigs where the fairies can sleep at night if they want to. Simon and Malcolm see me and run over. They whisper to each other, then they dig a hole in the red dirt where the rabbits have been burrowing.

'Betcha not game to wee into this hole!' Simon says.

'Yes I can, but I don't want to.'

'See,' he says, pulling his shorts down, 'you haven't got a cock like we have, but maybe you can wee out of your belly button 'cause you're a girl.'

'I don't want to!'

'See if you can,' Malcolm says, pulling his shorts down too. 'That way you don't have to take your pants off.'

I pull my skirt up and lie with my stomach over the hole and try to push the wee out of my belly button. Nothing comes out, but I wet my pants. I jump up before I make a puddle on the ground, and pull my skirt down. Simon stands over the hole and wees into it, then Malcolm does, and they run away laughing. I go behind the shed and wee on the ground.

In the gully past the windmill, there are big caves and steep sides like cliffs. The boys fight each other with catapults and stick guns. Simon chases Malcolm down the riverbank, and sees me sitting under a tree watching the river. He grabs me and drags me back up to the cave, and ties me up with long pieces of grass and vines from the riverbank.

'You're my hostage! Malcolm,' he yells. 'I've got Anna tied up. You'll have to fight me to rescue her.'

'Lemme go! Lemme go!' I wail.

But Simon laughs and jumps down into the gully waving his gun at Malcolm, who's running up the bank. 'Rattattattattat! You're dead!'

While his back's turned, I pull off the ties and run away.

*

The woolshed is bigger than the house with long boards polished smooth by men's feet and oil from the wool that is swept across the floor. When shearing time is on, it's noisy and smelly and warm. The engine chugs and sputters and the shearers' tackle hums as they work, racing to get their tally up. Each shearer has a station where a long cord hangs down with a handpiece on the end of it. The man grabs a sheep from the pen and drags it to his station, then sets the sheep on its bottom resting against his legs and starts shearing its belly. I love that first bit when the cutter slices through the dirty grey wool and it starts to fall away like an old rag, showing a velvety white belly. Sometimes the sheep wriggles or kicks and the cutter slips and the white under-wool turns bright pink. Dad says a good shearer works fast but doesn't cut the sheep too much. Little cuts are OK, big cuts have to be washed with a brush dipped in some smelly stuff, and if it keeps bleeding it has to be sewn up with a big sharp needle and some black thread. If a man makes too many big cuts, Dad gets angry.

After the shearing is over for the day, the boys chase each other in and out of the pens and hide behind the wool press.

I run over and climb on a fat bale of wool trussed up and branded ready to sell. 'I'm the king of the castle 'n' you're the dirty rascal!'

'Yah! You're just a girl! You can't be king!' Simon pushes me.

I land on my hands and knees and start to cry. 'Pig! I'll tell Mum!'

'Cry baby! Cry baby! You're just a stupid little girl!'

The boys go into a corner and whisper. They run outside and close the big wooden double doors that open out onto the loading bay. The doors close with a bar on the outside and I can't push them open.

'Ha-de-haha! If ya wanna get out, yer'll haveta say the magic word!' Simon yells through the gaps in the door.

I throw myself at the doors and try to push them open. That doesn't work so I sit down again. I could run out through the engine shed or sheep pens or out the back way through the mustering yards but they told me that there are ghosts of dead roustabouts and shearers under the floor at the back of the shed waiting to come out at night. I hear a shuffling noise near the shearers' stations. Pale yellow eyes stare at me from the shadows and a shearer's gear swings in a rhythmic pattern. A ghost shearer is shearing ghost sheep.

'Lemme out! Lemme out! Or I'll tell Mum on you!'

'Telltaletattletit! Say the magic word and we'll let you out!'

'What is it?'

There is whispering on the other side of the doors then Simon speaks through the round peephole above the bar. 'What ya haveta do is suck Malcolm's thumb 'cause 'e hurt it. He's gonna poke it through this hole and ya have ta suck it till it's better! Then we'll tell ya the word.'

A shiny purple thing with a slit in the end of it thrusts through the hole. The shuffling starts again behind me.

'Gowon! Suck it. It's sore.'

I put my mouth close to the door and begin to suck. It smells like when I wet my pants.

It slides back through the hole.

The floorboards behind me creak.

'Well! What's the word? You promised!'

Simon's voice growls, 'Cock!'

'Cock,' I whisper.

The doors swing open and Simon and Malcolm run off giggling into the bend.

Everything looks strange. The moon is hanging low in the sky and the trees in the bend shine like slimy ghosts.

I run as fast as I can to the kitchen, where Mum is getting the dinner ready. I sit near her in the kitchen and watch her pull the roast out of the oven and put it on a plate at the side of the stove while she makes the gravy.

She looks at me while she's stirring the gravy. 'You look pale, Anna. Are you all right?'

'Yes, Mum. But the boys shut me in the woolshed. I was scared, because it was getting dark. They wouldn't let me out till I said the magic word.'

She frowns. 'What was the magic word?'

'I don't want to say it.'

'Hmmph!' Mum looks at the clock and pulls the dish of vegetables out of the oven. 'The wretches. I'll talk to them later. Go and call them in, Anna. I want them to find Daddy and tell him dinner's ready. He's probably down yarning with the shearers in their hut.'

After dinner, she takes me out to the front veranda while the boys are drying the dishes. 'Darling, I want you to move into the little room off my bedroom to sleep. You're getting too big to sleep on the veranda.'

'Why, Mum? Why can't I sleep out here like the boys do?'

'Because they're big boys and they go to school now, and I want you to sleep where I can keep an eye on you.'

'But I like sleeping on the veranda!'

Martha takes a big breath and breathes out with a sigh. 'Just do as I say, Anna. You'll soon be seven, and you need to learn to be modest and behave like a little lady. Girls are different from boys, and you can't be a little tomboy and play rough games like they do.'

'Why not?'

'When you're older, you'll understand. For now, you must do as I say. Now take the little lamp from the living room and move your bedclothes into the little room. I'll help you make the bed after dinner.'

*

Next day, Mum sits me on her knee after she's finished the morning baking. 'Now, Anna, I want to tell you a story.'

'What about?'

'How babies are made. When a man and a woman love each other and get married, they want to have children.'

'How do they?'

Simon and Malcolm told me that Dad rescued me from under a gumtree. A crow had stolen me from another family who lived on the other side of the plains and when Dad shot at him with his twenty-two rifle the crow dropped me and flew away.

Mum uses some words I haven't heard before. I don't want to say them. I don't want to grow up and do that. I look down at my hands and shift my bottom on Mum's lap. I want to get down, but Mum is holding me tight.

'Doesn't it hurt?'

'Not if the man and woman love each other, because they want it to happen.' Mum drops her arms and pushes some hair off her face. She looks up at the clock. 'Heavens! I'd better check the scones.'

'Can I go and play?'

'Yes, darling.'

I run outside.

*

The grapevines are bare now but in summer they are loaded with sweet green muscatels and purple lady's fingers. Dad ties brown paper bags round the bunches so the birds don't get them. At the end of the kitchen garden is a big juniper bush and between it and the rose trees is a secret space just big enough for me to crawl into and hide.

Some mornings, I help the boys dig up spadefuls of worms, fat, shiny pink and wriggling. I watch while they stick hooks into them and throw lines into the river and wait for bites. The cod and perch are swimming round deep down. They probably know that the wriggly thing dangling above them is a trick. Maybe the only ones that take the bait are silly or too young to know better.

'There are old man cod swimming round down there that're bigger than you, Holly,' Dad says. He calls me Holly, Polly, Shorty, Stumpy, Hook, Pook… When he's in a bad mood, he calls me Anna. Once, he caught a huge cod in a net. He cut it into fillets and we ate some fresh. He salted the rest. We all got tired of eating salt fish.

I like fresh cod. The flesh is sweet and firm. Mum makes us eat bread or potato if we swallow one of the fine, small bones; she says it will wrap around the sharp point and stop it sticking into your stomach wall.

Once, I saw Dad pick Mum up and swing her round like a little girl. He said he had some good news to tell her. I wonder if she will have another baby. Maybe she's too old. Or maybe she doesn't want one.

I've never seen them with no clothes on. Making babies must be something that they only do when no one is looking. I put my hand inside my bloomers and feel between my legs. It's soft and wet and warm. I'm supposed to keep it covered and not touch it. Mum always scolds me if she sees me touching myself. But…they must have done it sometimes because they've got five kids.

Once, I walked into the bathroom when David was home on holidays. He was having a shower, singing at the top of his voice. There were fat white rolls around his middle. Mum told me that he was teased at school by the other boys and some of them tied him up and stuck the rolls together with sap from the fig tree. Hanging between his legs was a big reddish-purple thing. He covered it up and roared at me to get out. I ran out and stood outside the bathroom window on a box, trying to see in.

He started to sing again and I yelled, 'Ya sound like an elephant with a stomach ache!'

'Go away or I'll call Mum!'

I suppose he'll make babies with someone when he grows up and leaves home.

Making babies must feel like when I wet my pants. Maybe having a baby feels like when you have to do a big poo and it won't come out until you push really hard. What if it won't come out?

I can smell the juniper bush. It feels soft and springy and ticklish, a bit like an old toothbrush. There are lots of knobbly shiny nuts on it. I try to open them to see what's inside. I nibble one but it's bitter and I spit it out.

In spring and summer, one of the rose bushes has white flowers and the other has red but the bees get them mixed up so that white flowers are streaked with pink and red ones with white. Next to the roses is a lilac bush. In spring it has masses of pale purple flowers with white centres and a sweet musky smell. At the end of the bed is a crepe myrtle. It has pink and mauve blossoms all crumpled up like crushed silk.

Mum's voice calls me from the kitchen and I can smell freshly baked scones. A finger of sunlight pokes through a hole in the clouds and a magpie sings in the silver gum at the bottom of the garden. I jump up and brush the juniper needles off my skirt and run up the path to the house.

Drowning

There is something wrong this summer. Dad often takes Bess and the sulky and disappears for the rest of the day and sometimes the night. In the afternoons, Mum lies out on the veranda in her swinging canvas chair with a wet cloth on her forehead and sometimes I hear her crying. I haven't heard her cry before. I've seen her cross and tired when one of us does something wrong or Dad comes home late, and I've heard her shout at him sometimes. I wish she wouldn't cry. She always knows what to do to fix things, and stops the boys being mean to me if she's near, and sometimes she still takes me on her knee like when I was little and sings to me or tells me stories. I remember when I was very little she used to call me Lilly-Bud-Boo and rock me in her arms.

One day, Dad stays home because the windmill pump isn't working and we are running out of water. A pipe runs from the windmill into a deep hole in the river. He gets Malcolm to help him. I'm playing on the river-bank trying to teach tricks to Bruiser, the collie puppy. One of my dreams is to have a circus of acrobats and performing animals and travel from town to town all over the world.

'Siddup, Bruiser!' I hold up my apple core, wanting him to sit up on his back legs and beg for it.

Bruiser sits on his haunches, one ear flopping, one pricked up, and scratches his floppy ear with his hind leg.

'Anna!' Dad yells. 'Leave that bloody pup alone and go and get me a pot of white paint.'

I run to the shed, find the pot of paint and start back with it. It is heavy and I walk carefully towards the top of the riverbank, stepping over fallen logs and avoiding rabbit holes.

'Hurry up! Yer as slow as a bloody wet week!' He is in the muddy water on the edge of the bank bending over the pipe, wrapping some white stuff round it.

Malcolm is treading water in the deep part, holding the pipe up out of the water.

I begin to run and trip over a large log lying halfway down the bank. The pot of paint flies out of my hands.

I fall through the water into the deep green.

I'm sinking down

down

down. My eyes are open.

I see only green so dark it's almost black.

The river's swallowing me. I sink into its depths.

I hear

shouting.

'GedinthereMalcolmyabloodyfoolnpullerout!'

The water sucks me

down

down down.

This is it. Dad will be sorry and Mum will cry.

A splash.

I'm pulled by the hair, landing like a fish on the bank. Blinded by the sun I cough up the river.

I want to go back.

I don't want to breathe air.

He picks me up. He's red and angry. 'There, you're all right now. Go an tell your mother and don't you dare cry!'

I run to the house, water dripping from my best blue dress splashed with white paint. Mum's on the veranda sewing. I stand in front of her and try to laugh.

She stops treadling. 'Darling! How dreadful.' She jumps up. 'You poor child, what on earth has happened?'

I gaze at my feet. A dark puddle is spreading around me.

Bad dreams

A wall of water comes roaring down the river bed, overflowing the edges, pushing down trees, sweeping away sheep and horses. The Burrinjuck Dam has burst. It is rushing towards me. I cannot move.

When Mum has the wireless on, I hear a man saying that the scientists say the world is heading for another Ice Age. The last one ended about ten thousand years ago. They say the ice will spread from the North and South Poles and cover most of the earth. I imagine the ice appearing, frosting the flat edges of the horizon, creeping, creeping, till it covers all the paddocks.

One night, I wake from a dream that a big ram is chasing me across a paddock with no fences and nowhere I can hide from his sharp horns. I hear voices shouting, thumps and bumps. I creep out to the back veranda and crouch on one of the empty beds there. I smell something sickly like burnt custard. There's a window without glass opening into the room where Dad sleeps. I crawl over and peer through the gaps between the curtains. He has a bottle in his hands and he's waving it around as he shouts:

'Lemme alone! Bloody woman! I'll do wharilike!'

'Henry – give me the bottle. You've had too much already!' Mum grabs the bottle and he lurches away.

He falls across the bed, banging his head on the bed-end. She yanks the bottle from his hands. She runs over to the outside window, pushes it up, and throws the bottle out into the rose bushes. She turns round and walks towards the door.

'Curseya! Yer'll be shorry for thish…' he mumbles and closes his eyes.

She comes looking for me. I jump into bed.

'You poor child. Come and sleep with me.' She picks me up and carries me into her own bed.

I wake up crying from a bad dream. The sky was green, a lurid green like rotten lettuce. Orange darts of flame were shooting across it. The earth shuddered and the ground in front of me cracked open. Mum was standing on my side of the crack, holding out her arms to me. Dad was standing at the other side calling me – 'Holly! Holly!' I wanted to be with him, but I knew Mum would die alone if I did. I stepped back from the crack to be close to her and as I did the earth split apart. A huge chasm opened up and swallowed the ground where Dad was standing. He fell, his arms waving like insects' feelers, and as he fell he made a tiny shrill chirping cry like a cricket, 'Holly! Holly!'

'Mum, what will happen to Dad? Is he going away?'

Mum holds me and shushes me and hums an old lullaby. I snuggle into her arms. I don't remember ever sleeping with her before.

Behind the orange tree

Dad's getting ready to go out again, and Mum's looking cross.

She sends me out to the garden. 'Go and get me some salad vegetables, Anna. Your father hasn't been looking after the garden. But there should be a few things that have survived.'

She gives me a colander and walks out to the shed, where Dad's harnessing Bess. The Chev has broken down again.

I pick a couple of tomatoes and a cucumber that was hiding under the leaves, and find a lettuce that hasn't gone to seed. I can hear their voices in the shed, so I go over and stand behind the orange tree where they can't see me.

'Henry, this has to stop. We can't live like this.'

'What has to stop?'

'You know what I mean. It's not just that you're never here. It's not just the drinking. I know why you're drinking.'

'Do you, Mrs Know-all. Why's that?'

'Because you're seeing that woman, the cook on Wyalgie. That's why you go over there all the time.'

'Is it indeed? I'll tell you why I go. Because I have to talk to someone.'

'You used to talk to me, Henry.'

'Yes, until I got tired of being carped at all the time. Whatever I do, it's wrong in your book. A man needs to relax, to have a laugh. All you talk about is what's wrong.'

'Henry, that's not true!' Mum's voice softens. 'We've been through so much together. Drought, the Depression, dust storms, losing the flock, bringing up five children, and now, just when things are starting to look up, you're giving up.'

'I'm not giving up!' His voice gets louder. 'I just need a break. A break from work, a break from being preached to.'

I can hear the wheels of the sulky creaking. He must be putting Bess between the shafts.

'Henry,' Mum says, in a voice she uses when she's giving orders, 'I'm tired of your excuses. I'm going to take Anna to Wollongong to stay with Irene for a while, and I'll look for a job in Sydney for term time, while the boys are at school. I hope you'll come to your senses while we're away.'

'Do as you like,' he says. 'I don't care. Leave me to do all the work. Walk away from it all.'

'Henry, grow up. You haven't got your mother's skirts to hide behind any more. We took this place on to live together and raise a family and make an honest living. We've been through so much together. Be careful you don't throw it all away.'

He curses and slaps the reins on Bess's rump. 'Gee up, Bess.'

Mum's footsteps are coming near.

I run towards her. 'Mum! Are we going away?'

'Yes, darling. I'll write to Irene and tell her we're coming for a holiday.'

'But Mum…what about Dad?'

'Your father can look after himself for a while. He's perfectly capable of it.'

She looks cross and tired, but she takes my hand and we walk back to the kitchen together.

Wollongong

Aunt Irene lives in Wollongong, in the house she and Mum were born in. It's a weatherboard cottage painted white with green trimmings. The front has a gable and a wooden veranda, and inside there is a long hallway with rooms on either side. The garden is big but not as interesting as Arendal. It is mostly grass with a few bushes round the edges. The best part is the paddock at the back behind the garage. Part of it is fenced off for chooks and the rest is wild with long grass and blackberry bushes and a mulberry and a fig tree.

There is a laneway leading to the street that I walk along to the butcher's shop. The paspalum grows tall beside the track, and its sticky seeds cling to my socks. The butcher's shop is up the hill at the corner of two streets. I read out the list Aunt Irene gave me, and wait while the butcher cuts up the meat and wraps it in white paper. He hands me all the parcels and I put them in the string bag and count the money out from the purse. Then I'm allowed to go to the corner store in the next street and buy an ice cream with the change.

When I bring the meat home, Aunt Irene puts it away in the fridge, except for the cat's meat. She sets a board on the kitchen table and chops up the steak and kidneys while the cats sit watching. She has seven cats. The biggest is Squash, a fat old tabby tomcat. He sleeps on my bed at night. He is heavy and smells damp. He licks his fur a lot with a wet squashy noise and when he is sleeping he snuffles and snores.

Aunt Irene goes out every morning early before I get up and drives around in her car to places where the stray cats are and leaves meat and milk for them.

One day, I come home and find her in the bathroom kneeling behind a bucket of water.

'Moggy had seven kittens today,' she says, looking up from the bucket. One hand is holding a tiny sleek black body with twiggy legs and pink paws under the water. It squirms for a few seconds then is still.

'We can't keep them all. There are too many unwanted cats in the world already.' She pulls out the limp bundle and reaches for another soft handful from the box next to her. 'I shut Moggy outside. Go and find her and give her a cuddle. Tell her I'm keeping the tortoiseshell one for her.'

I run outside and find Moggy under the house near the bathroom miaowing in a croaky voice. I crawl in under the cobwebby beams and put my arms round her but she scratches me and jumps out of my arms.

I go down to the paddock and climb into the mulberry tree. I can still hear Moggy.

When I go inside, Aunt Irene is in the kitchen chopping up meat for the cats.

'Where's Moggy?' I say, stepping past the waiting cats.

'She's with the tortoiseshell kitten. I've buried the others.' She chops the last of the meat and puts it in the dishes lined up on the floor. 'I had a letter from your mother today. She's decided to stay in Sydney and teach at a boys' high school. She wants to brush up her teaching skills and earn some money, and she needs a rest from the farm and all that hard work and worry.'

Her curls bob up and down as she chops. She wears her brown hair in a short bob, and goes to the hairdresser every Saturday to have it set. She comes home with her hair all flat and shiny under a net, with bobby pins fastening tight little curls round the edge and butterfly clips on the sides and back making sharp waves in a choppy sea.

She puts the knife in the sink and turns to the table. 'She wants you to stay with me and go to school here for a while.'

'But…when will she come back?'

'She'll be here for the holidays. Then I expect she'll decide what to do, whether to go back to Arendal or not.' She places the bowls on the floor, one in front of each cat, and washes her hands at the sink.

'But…what about Dad? What will he do if we don't go back?'

'Your father can look after himself.' She sniffs and dries her hands, then picks up the kettle and fills it with water. 'I'll take you to town tomorrow to buy a uniform, and you'll start school next Monday.'

'What class will I be in?'

'I don't know. They'll probably give you some tests to see where you're up to. It will be good for you to be with children your own age.' She sets the kettle on the gas hob and strikes a match to light the burner. The flame is blue and the gas sounds like a soft wind blowing across the plains.

I wish I were home with Dad again. I wonder what he's doing. I hope he's getting the broken things fixed so Mum won't be so cross with him and we can go back.

Aunt Irene is polite to me, but she isn't much fun. She's always doing something, polishing and cleaning the floors, or practising the piano, or feeding the cats, and I try to stay out of her way. She doesn't seem to take much notice of what I do as long as I don't make a mess. She loves her cats more than me. Mum made me work hard and do housework but I know she loves me and she needs my help. Sometimes when she wasn't busy, she'd sit me on her knee and read to me, or show me how to knit, or tell me stories about my grandparents, who were all dead before I was born. I'm worried about her. She must be lonely without me and the boys and the house and the garden and the bend and the galahs and the animals and the river.

Schooldays

On Monday, I get up early and polish my new brown lace-up shoes and put on my navy skirt and white blouse. Aunt Irene is up early too. After her cat run, she practises the piano for half an hour. She used to teach French in high school, but Mum said she found the children too hard to control, so she switched to teaching kindergarten. Usually I wake to the sound of her practising scales and thumping out nursery rhymes.

My hair has grown back down to the top of my shoulders since I cut one of my plaits off and Vera cut the other side short to match. Last night, I went to bed with rags tied in it to make curls. It is fine and wavy, not thick and curly like Vera's. When I've brushed it, Aunt Irene pulls a bunch of hair together on either side of my face and ties it back with a white ribbon.

After porridge and toast, I make a sandwich, peanut butter and mashed banana, and put it in a brown paper bag with an apple. I put the bag and my new exercise books, pencils, rubber and sharpener in the leather school bag Aunt bought for me. It is shaped like a saddlebag and has a long strap that goes over my shoulder.

We walk along the street to the primary school two blocks away. Past the doctor's house opposite with its big garden and tennis court and tall trees. Past the brick house with a garden of roses and lots of other flowers that remind me of Dad's flower beds. I can hear the noise of the children before we get near the school.

There are rows of brown wooden buildings and two huge playgrounds covered in bitumen. The boys are in one, the girls in the other. They are running, laughing, calling out to each other; girls are skipping and playing hopscotch and some boys are kicking a football around. I've never seen so many children in my life.

I wish I was at home with Dad doing my correspondence lessons. Why didn't Mum leave me with him, if she had to get away for a while and get a job? I can cook now. I could keep house for him. He'd have to stay home then and look after me. And I like doing correspondence. I like getting the fat brown envelope every couple of weeks, and opening it, and seeing what my lessons are. I like the geography lessons; the last one I did was about clouds.

> Red sky at morning
> shepherd's warning
> Red sky at night
> shepherd's delight
> Mackerel sky
> not long wet, not long dry
> Mare's tails and mackerel sky
> rain before twenty-four hours have gone by.

The cumulus clouds are my favourite. Great cloud-palaces piled up on the horizon, rounded and billowing, purply-grey at the bottom with creamy frothy peaks at the top like one of Mum's lemon meringue pies. I miss the open skies, even the summer sky, pale as dead sheep's bones.

The headmistress puts me in a class with over thirty kids. 'This is a mixed class, second and third. Some children in this class turn eight this year, some turn nine. You're a year younger, Anna, but the tests you've done show you're ready for the work. Your mother has done a good job,' she says as she shepherds me in.

'Good morning, Mrs Miller. Good morning, children. You have a new classmate. This is Anna Anderson, all the way from Hay in the outback. She's been doing correspondence lessons till now, so this is her first time in a big classroom. Make sure you make her welcome and show her where things are.'

Rows of faces stare at me. Boys on one side of the room, girls on the other. They all look bigger. I'm small for my age. Dad sometimes calls me Shorty or Stumpy. I want to run out the door and catch the train home. The teacher tells me to sit next to Robyn, a tall blonde girl.

The first lesson is Reading, and Mrs Miller calls out the names of a couple of the girls and boys to read aloud. Robyn shares her reader with me.

'Anna Anderson! Stand up and show us how well you can read.'

The story is about a boy and girl who go to the seaside for a holiday with their mother. The words are easy, and I read it in my best voice.

'Now that is lovely. If I were sick, I'd want Anna to read to me.'

A boy in the row across from me snorts and pulls a face at me.

'Thank you, Anna. Sit down. Now, Peter! Since you're so smart, read the next page please.'

At recess they line up for little bottles of free milk. I give mine to Robyn. I don't like the cold sickly taste or slimy feeling it leaves in my mouth. We play tag and I fall and hurt my knee on the bitumen. There is a hole in my knee with dirt and gravel in it and a bloody flap of skin hanging down. Warm blood trickles down my leg onto my white sock. Robyn takes me to the nurse, who cleans out the dirt and gravel and dabs the hole with stinging red stuff then puts a band-aid over it.

At lunchtime, Robyn asks me to sit with her and her friend Pam to eat lunch. When we finish our sandwiches, we play jacks with coloured plastic knucklebones. Most of the jacks fall off when I try to catch them on the back of my hand, they are so slippery and my hands are small. Mum used to save knucklebones from the hogget legs for me. I've got a whole set at home dyed the colours of the rainbow.

I wonder how Mum likes teaching all boys. Some of the boys here are big and rough. But there's one boy in my class I like; he sits at the back and he's good at arithmetic. Mrs Miller got him to help me with a sum I couldn't do this morning. He has blue eyes and dark hair like Dad's. His name is Murray. Murray Sainsbury. I repeat his name over and over so I can always remember it. When he smiles at me, I feel warm all over.

I wonder if Mum is missing Dad. I hope she'll come soon and we can go home. I think of Curly; he must have grown really big since I left. I hope Dad hasn't sold him. He says poddy lambs are a pest when they grow up because they break through the fences and lead the other sheep astray. He says the best thing to do with them is sell them off with the other wethers. But I know if that happens he'll just end up on someone's table.

I come in behind the other girls after a trip to the toilet.

Robyn is whispering to a big girl in the desk in front. She looks at me and grins. 'We're talking about bleeding. Do you know about it?'

'You mean when you cut yourself or fall over?' I remember how warm the blood felt as it trickled down my leg.

'No, silly!' Robyn says with a giggle. 'Hasn't your mum told you?'

Mrs Miller walks in and we all stand up.

I wish I was back home. I wasn't lonely there. Here I'm surrounded by kids and I don't know how to talk to them.

Weekends

Betty Simpson is my weekend friend. She is the top girl in the class, and sits in the back row near Murray. She is tall with smooth short brown hair, creamy skin and brown eyes. She is quiet and doesn't hang around the boys like Robyn does. On Saturday morning, after I've been to the butcher's and swept the floor and helped Aunt Irene hang the washing on the line, I walk down to Betty's house at the other end of town.

Mr and Mrs Simpson have funny English accents and own a cake shop and they are always at work except on Sundays. During the week, they get up early in the mornings and leave Betty and her sister Susan to get themselves to school. The house is always in a mess and meals are not at set times. They eat buns and cakes and pies left over from the shop. It's a nice change from Aunt Irene's, where everything is neat and tidy and runs by the clock and the cats rule the house.

Aunt says Betty and Susan are spoiled. They have a whole wardrobe full of dresses and shoes, and every season their parents buy new ones for them. They each have a lovely silver brush and comb and mirror set and crystal dishes with necklaces and bracelets in them and real perfume in a crystal bottle with a puffer spray. They are allowed to wear lipstick and powder at the weekends, and Susan goes out with boys.

When I visit, we play games of Monopoly which go on all weekend and read comics and go to the Saturday afternoon movies and eat ice cream in cardboard cups with a wooden spoon. On Sundays, Mr Simpson takes us for drives in his big shiny Humber car with brown leather seats and a radio. We drive up Bulli Pass round the hairpin bends and have Devonshire tea in the café at the top looking out over the green rolling hills to the scribbled shapes of Wollongong with the sapphire ocean sparkling beyond. He takes us to the blowhole at Kiama and we stand on the rocks while the water sucks back then bursts with an 'oomph!' in a white cloud from the hole up into the air wetting us with the spray. Afterwards we walk along the beach dipping our toes and fingers in rock pools, tiny worlds where anemones and little crabs and shellfish live.

It is a magical world but it is not mine. I miss the sky, the plains, the sheep, the bend of trees, the river…

Beach

I try to learn at school and play with the others. They all have mothers and fathers and homes of their own, and the ones I play with have lots of toys and clothes and family outings at the weekend. Sometimes, Robyn asks me to go to the beach with her after school. We meet outside her house, which is close to the beach, and walk down to the pool, a piece of ocean enclosed by cement. The surf washes over the wall when the tide is in and sometimes a big wave comes and floods the surrounding rocks. At the ocean end, the pool is too deep for me to stand up but when the tide is out I feel safe because I can hang onto the wall. I breathe in the salty seaweedy smell of the ocean and my fingers probe the little shelled creatures clinging to the seaweed-coated cement. Robyn is doing laps, her long golden legs and arms splashing in and out of the water. We lie on our spread-out towels on the rocks by the pool. I am freckled and pale and my skin turns bright pink in the scorching sun.

A few days later, my skin blisters and peels off in sheets. Then I go to the beach again with Robyn and we lie on the sand and I get burnt again. Robyn has a new swimsuit, a navy blue Jansen that shows off her small round breasts and slim waist. The elastic in my bubble costume is loose and saggy. I have no breasts and my stomach doesn't go in at the waist like Robyn's.

'Eh Robyn, owyadoin'? Wanna come out and catch a wave?' a tall blond boy with muscly arms and chest calls out as he jogs past on his way to the water.

'Yeah, wait for me!' She jumps up, scattering sand over me, and runs beside him.

I sit and watch as they move out through the breaking waves until they are just shapes bobbing up and down among the other surfers.

I jump up and run to the water. I move through the waves as they break. I can't stand up. Perhaps I will be sucked out to sea by a current and sink into the dark green depths.

Return

School holidays come at last and Mum arrives. She looks thinner and her hair has more grey in it. She and Aunt Irene are in the kitchen getting dinner, and I creep near the door so I can hear what they are saying.

'Have you decided if you're going back to Arendal?' Aunt Irene asks.

'I don't know. I don't know. I want to, but…'

'Have you heard from him?'

'Not for a couple of weeks. Then it was just a short note with my spare reading glasses I'd asked him to send.'

'What about Simon and Malcolm? Are they at home?'

'No, I arranged for them to stay with their friends for the holidays. I don't want them at home doing all the work while he goes off and wastes time with that woman.'

'What does he have to say for himself?'

'Oh, nothing much. Just that there's been no rain and he's hand-feeding the sheep.'

'Do you think he's still seeing her?'

'Of course. I hoped he would think better of it once we were away, realise what he risks losing, but he's given me no reason to hope for a change of heart.'

'Well, Martha, if you don't go back, he can do what he likes, and let the farm go to rack and ruin, let everything you've worked so hard for go to waste.'

'I know. I suppose I'll have to have it out with him.'

I run outside to the bottom paddock and climb the mulberry tree. The chooks are scratching under the tree and having dust baths. We don't have chooks at home any more; Dad killed them one by one when they stopped laying.

*

On the South-west Mail, we pull out of Central Station and I watch the lights of factories and houses flash past. Mum and I have a carriage to ourselves so we can each have a whole bench seat to sleep on. But Mum gets to me sit next to her.

'Anna, I don't know how things will be when we go home.'

'Why, Mum? Will Dad be there?'

'Yes, but I don't have much hope that things will have changed.' She looks at me for a moment, then turns her head and looks out the window. 'You know he's been keeping company with a woman at Wyalgie. The cook.' Her voice is tight.

'Why?' I said. 'Doesn't he love you any more?'

She takes a deep breath and turns her face to me. 'I think so, Anna, but sometimes I wonder. I think he's just tired of the struggle and tired of working so hard and he wants to spend time with someone who doesn't remind him of all the things that need to be done. I think he knows she's not my equal, but your father's never been very particular about the company he keeps. He likes anyone who'll talk to him and swap yarns and jokes. He's all right when he's on his own, he's a hard worker, but he gets led astray.'

'But Mum, will he go away?' I don't want him to, I want things to go back to how they were.

'I don't know, Anna. But what I do know is if we don't go back he'll just do as he pleases and the place will get more run-down and we won't be able to make a living from it. So we'll have to leave anyway.'

'I don't want to leave!' I say, burying my face in her arm.

She puts her arm around me and holds me close. 'I don't either, darling. My time in the city has brought that home to me more than ever. I miss it so much.'

I snuggle up to her for a while until she gets me to stretch out on the opposite seat so I can sleep. I nestle down with a cushion under my head and a rug over me and think of the little sandy beach we swim at and the river's song.

I wake up when we stop at a station and the guard is calling out, and she's still sitting up straight staring out the window.

*

Mum and Dad haven't spoken a word since we climbed into the sulky at the siding. Mum's arms are folded across her chest and her hat is pulled down to shade her eyes. Dad stares straight ahead, slapping the reins against Bess's sides every now and then to make her go faster.

Clouds of red dust swirl behind us. The paddocks are flat and empty, dry and brown except for patches of grey-green, the same as they are at the end of summer every year. But it all looks drier and emptier after the greens and blues of the coast.

When we reach the house, I jump out and run to my favourite spots in the garden. The flower beds are full of dead plants. Even the roses and flowering shrubs look straggly and starved of water. I run to greet the dogs. They are ecstatic to see me but they are thin and hungry-looking.

I hear Mum's angry voice calling me and walk slowly towards the house.

'What's wrong? What've I done?'

'Nothing. It's not you, it's Daddy. He's gone off to Wyalgie, and look! This is all he's left us to eat!' She thrusts a tin with some mouldy scones at me and starts searching through storage bins on the shelves. Her hair is falling out of its bun, and her face is flushed. In the last container, she finds some flour.

'Go out to the safe and see if there's anything in there we can eat. Some meat or butter. Hurry up!'

There is only a shank bone with a bit of salted meat left on it, and a scrap of butter in the dish.

'Well! That's better than nothing. Go and see if there are any vegetables in the garden.'

The beds are choked with weeds but I find a tomato bush half-dead with a couple of small ripe tomatoes on it and a lettuce that hasn't gone to seed.

Mum gets me to help her clean out the range, coated with dust and spider webs and choked with ashes. Our meal is a few scraps of meat, salad and some damper.

Mum doesn't say much at teatime. Her eyes are red and she looks old and tired. I'm not hungry, but she makes me eat what's on my plate. We wash up and she sends me to bed straight after. No stories tonight.

I lie in the dark and close my eyes. Dad will come home and say he's sorry and he's going to stay home and work hard from now on. Mum will make a pot of tea and they'll sit and talk like they used to about the farm and the sheep and the wool crop and the garden. He'll tell her he loves her, he always has, and she'll let him hug and kiss her and they'll be friends again. Tomorrow, Dad will be out in the garden whistling and digging up the weeds and when I go outside he'll put his arm round me and take me to see the new garden bed he's made and tell me what he's going to plant in it.

Dad goes

'You've ruined our lives! How could you let yourself go like this?' Mum's voice cracks, and she sobs, 'What on earth do you see in her?'

I sit under the juniper bush with my hands over my ears, but I can still hear them.

'She's good fun to be with. Not like you!' Dad's voice gets louder as he pushes open the screen door and slams it behind him. 'You never open your mouth without finding fault with someone,' he yells. 'I'm sick and tired of trying to live up to your standards.'

'You may as well go then! Go and be done with us.'

There is a crash of broken crockery.

'You're no use round here. This place is falling apart, I could run it better myself.' The screen door slams again and she runs after him as he walks towards the shed. 'Go to your tart, and see how well she wears when times are hard,' she screams.

I've never heard Mum scream before.

I run down to the river bend. I can still hear their voices, tangled and cross and full of hate but I can't hear the words. The river slides past and I listen to its song. But I keep hearing their voices, they drown out the river and I put my hand over my ears. I wish I could be a fairy godmother and change everything back to how it was. I don't want to lose Dad. I don't want Mum to cry and scream and worry all the time. I wish I could just wake up and find it's all been a bad dream. I used to think I was dreaming and one day I'd wake up and find this world isn't real. I wish it weren't.

*

'What are you doing, Mum?'

'Nothing, darling. Just looking for something.' She is at Dad's desk opening drawers. She pulls out a writing pad and holds it up to the light. She screws up her eyes behind her glasses. 'Here, Anna. Your eyes are better than mine. See how there are marks on the paper from writing on the page that's been torn off? Can you see what the words were?'

I can see the ghosts of his strong, curly writing.

'Darling…hell…be with you…leave soon…'

Mum grabs the pad from me and throws it back into the desk. She makes a choking noise and slumps down on the bed.

'What is it, Mum? What's Dad done?'

'It's Mrs Dalton, the cook at Wyalgie Station. I think he plans to go away with her.'

I haven't seen her cry like this before, as if the sun has dried up all her tears and every sob has to tear its way through a mass of thorns and barbed wire.

'Doesn't he want to be with us any more, Mum?'

Mum takes a big breath and straightens her shoulders. 'I don't think Daddy knows what he wants. He's looking for an escape.' She pulls a hanky from her apron pocket and wipes her eyes and cheeks. 'This woman is just a way out. She's inferior to him.' She stands and walks towards the kitchen, stuffing the hanky in her pocket.

I follow her. 'What do you mean, inferior, Mum?'

'She's fat, she's common. Dolloping Dumbo Dalton. She can barely even read or write. But she's got her hooks into him, and he's besotted.'

'Besotted. What's that?'

Mum puts the kettle on, and I go outside to the apple tree. I nestle in the bowl of the trunk like I used to and try to let my mind float. But I remember once when Dad took me with him one time when he went to Wyalgie and he told me to wait for him in the Chev after we'd got some vegies from the Chinese gardener. I waited for ages and he didn't come so I went to look for him.

He was sitting on the back veranda outside the kitchen with her.

She was wearing bright red lipstick and she smelled musky. She was fat with red hair, curly and messy, and you could see the shape of her through her dress. Maybe she doesn't wear corsets like Mum does. Dad was sitting down near her and they were drinking beer and smoking. She laughed and leaned over to say something to him and her breasts wobbled and her stomach shook. He laughed and leaned back, blowing smoke rings, and she took another swig of beer. He stubbed his cigarette out and leaned over and said something in a low voice.

So that's who Dolloping Dumbo Dalton is. I wish I'd never seen her. I wish she were dead.

*

'Are you going away?' I ask.

Dad is at the bottom of the vegetable garden, digging in the turnip bed. He is bending over the spade. I can only see the side of his face, his red cheek and curved nose, his creased eye with a bit of blue showing, his mouth tight shut, his black hair brushed back, shiny like oil in a winter puddle of rain. He keeps digging.

'Yes, Holly – your mother and I – don't get on any more – I have to go,' he says in jerks as he works the spade in the soil, picks up the turnips and chucks them in the bag, plop, plop, plop.

'But Dad…I don't want you to go.'

He puts his spade down and turns towards me. He picks me up and presses his cheek against mine.

'Will I see you again? Will you come back?' I touch the side of his face, warm and wet.

A drop of sweat runs down his neck and disappears inside his shirt. He says nothing for a while, just stands with his arms wrapped round me, then puts me down and squats down beside me. He looks at the brown chopped-up earth. A pink worm slides around a clod and disappears underneath it.

'See, Holly, I don't know where I'm going and I might not have a house to live in for a while,' he says softly.

My nose bubbles. My throat is tight and sore.

'Now, Holly, go up to your mother. You have to look after her.' He brushes his hand across his eyes, mutters a curse, then straightens up and moves back to the row of turnips, picks up the spade again and starts to dig up another wilted plant.

I run away to the bend. I climb a big gum tree that hangs over the river. I blow my nose between my fingers and wipe the snot off on the gum leaves. I watch the ants trailing up and down the trunk. The ones going down are carrying bits of dead insect. The bits are bigger than they are. The cicadas shrill in my ears and I close my eyes.

When I open my eyes, the sun is getting low in the sky. I run up to the house. It is quiet and still and the rooms feel empty and lost like the ghost of a house. I go into Dad's room. The bed has been stripped. The wardrobe door is open and his clothes are gone except for a couple of old pairs of trousers and a khaki shirt. I rub my nose against the shirt and smell his tobacco and his sweat.

Mum is in the kitchen chopping an onion into tiny bits. Her face is crumpled and her hair is straggling out of the bun.

'Mum, has Dad gone?'

'Yes. He looked for you to say goodbye but he couldn't find you.' She looks at me then looks back at the chopping board. Her eyes are red. She sniffs and pulls a handkerchief out of her apron pocket and wipes it across her face. 'This onion is so strong!'

'Will he come back?'

'No, Anna. He's gone for good. He left this for you.' She blows her nose and reaches across to the window-sill and hands me an envelope.

In it is the mouth organ he used to play in the evenings after dinner and a folded piece of paper. I run outside and sit on the step. I unfold the paper.

'HOLLY I'M SORRY. I LOVE YOU.'

Every day, I go outside as soon as my jobs are done and walk through the home paddock up to the main road. I weep and weep, and play long rambling tunes on the mouth organ and watch the road. My tunes have no beginning and no end. The red line of the road cuts through the grey-green paddocks. Whenever a car or truck hums along it I hold my breath and hope it will turn into our gate.

When the rains come, I sit on a pile of sawdust near the wood heap and watch the deep brown waters rush by. Muddy cream bubbles swirl along the edge and get trapped in sticks and leaves and scum. A log floats past with a water rat and a snake clinging to it.

I don't want to live here any more. I wish I could die. I see myself falling in the river again, swept along until I go under. I see my mother pacing up and down the bank calling for me and my brothers diving in to find me.

But I'm here, he's gone, the boys are at school in Hay and David's in the city and Vera's in London and it's just Mum and me now. I can't leave her alone.

*

At night, we lie in our separate beds and the empty house echoes our breath. The windows rattle and the cedar taps on the tin roof. When mopokes call in the bend or a fox howls, I shiver and pull the blankets over my head. When Dad was here, I felt safe at night; I liked the night sounds, even when there were storms and the house shook and the roof creaked. I liked it when the rain made the tin roof sing and the wind howled at the windows. Now I hate it and just want the night to end.

The old woman who works on the plains at night, covering the ravaged earth with a woven mat of saltbush, is growing tired of her endless task. There are so many bare patches of soil. She remembers a time when the ground was covered with vegetation: a mixture of trefoil clover and tussocky wild grass, round prickle bush, and woody old man saltbush. In spring, there were pink and purple vetches, yellow bachelor's buttons, white and pink everlasting daisies, scarlet and purple desert peas. Weeping myall trees once graced the space above the embroidered plain, with their long, pointed grey-green leaves, yellow puffball flowers in summer and autumn, and wood that smelled of violets. The early settlers cut down most of the myall for posts to fence in their herds, and the cloven hooves of the sheep worked with the wind and the drought to erode the groundcover.

Now, the only annual that thrives is Paterson's Curse, with its rough hairy leaves and purple trumpet shaped flowers, crowding out all other plants in swaths of royal purple and bright green, poisoning horses and cattle if they feed on it for long.

She must do what she can. The creeping silvery saltbush that falls from her fingers stores water in its small round fleshy leaves, and the sheep love it. She works on with rhythmic movements of her hands, humming a tune that echoes the wind rustling the leaves of the river gums in the bend.

Alone

The air is dry and crackly like it will snap if you make a sudden movement. Last week they said on the wireless that a murderer escaped from a prison near the border not so far from here. I step out the back door and scan the bend behind the house looking for a telltale puff of smoke from a campfire or a figure moving furtively through the trees.

Mum won't be back from town for another hour or more. The clock on the mantelpiece says four o'clock. I've eaten lunch and washed up and don't feel like reading my book. I've done my correspondence lessons except for a few sums I'm not sure how to do.

I think over the list of jobs Mum left. I reckon I've done everything. I've fed the dogs, made the beds and swept the floors. I'll start cooking dinner later, fish hash from a tin of salmon mixed with chopped onions and herbs with breadcrumbs on top and dobs of butter. Mum will bring fresh meat home but it will be too late to cook it then. We don't kill our own sheep any more.

I walk out onto the front veranda and push open the screen door. The green canopy of the cedar tree calls me. I climb up high to a comfortable fork in the branches where I can see the road and the bends. There is a hush over the paddocks except for baby galahs crying in the big sugar gums at the edge of the garden. I hug my knees to my chest as I lean against the rough bark and close my eyes.

A wind comes up, shaking the poplar trees near the tank, rustling the cedar leaves, swaying the branches around me. The sun slices through the clouds and sends a shaft of violet light across the road. Thunder rumbles from the edge of the world and a spear of lightning shoots down to earth beyond the windmill in the far paddock.

Shimmering lines of fence posts wobble and disappear across flat dun-coloured plains. Down in the bend, birds call to each other and near the house the dogs howl.

A utility appears – a little blob with a tail moving along. I strain my eyes to see if it will turn into the home paddock but it doesn't. Maybe Mum isn't coming back from her trip to town.

I close my eyes again like I do when she is going through a gate or reversing or going over a culvert. So many times we end up bogged because she's skidded off the road in wet weather, stuck in the red mud, wheels churning, engine roaring. Sometimes she gets distracted and doesn't see a bump in the road or a pothole and loses control of the steering wheel and we end up in the ditch again.

I see her taking a turn too sharply and skidding off the road into a fence post. She's thrown out of the cabin. Her neck is twisted and dark red blood oozes from her mouth.

I see the funeral, a small procession of mourners. I walk by the coffin white-faced and silent.

I open my eyes. Fat blobs of rain are falling, leaving watermarks on the dusty leaves. It will soon be dark. I'll light the lamps and close the doors and hope the escaped prisoner doesn't come this way.

Broken down

Mum turns on the ignition and pushes the starter button but instead of the roar of the engine there is a strangled cough then silence. After a couple more tries, she gets out and raises the bonnet and I climb down. We stand and stare at the maze of the engine. She gets back into the cabin and tries to start the motor again. The dogs jump down from the tray and take shelter under the truck panting. A crow sits on the fence watching and rasps, 'Aargh…aaarrgh…aaaarrrgh!' and flies away.

'Damn and blast! Myall station has an outpost a couple of miles away,' she says slamming the bonnet down. 'We'll have to walk over and see if the boundary rider's there.'

We set off carrying the hessian water bag, which still has a few mouthfuls of cool water in it. The sun is well past the centre of the sky by the time we reach the timber and iron shack shaded by pepper trees. The shed and the dog kennel are empty.

'They must've gone into town,' Mum says. 'We'll have to wait for them to come back.'

We settle down on a couple of old canvas chairs on the front veranda and Mum closes her eyes. The dogs flop down near her, panting. I look around for a tap. There is one on the side of the tank but only a rusty dribble comes out. I go into the shed and fossick round till I find a half-empty lemonade bottle. I take it back to Mum.

'You don't know what's in it, Anna. It might be poisoned.' She sighs. 'No woman should have to live in these conditions. That poor soul! Fancy having to live out here with no river, hardly any rainwater, having to rely on bore water most of the time, no garden to speak of.' She turns her head and looks at the battered front door and cracked dirty windowpanes.

'Mum, what was it like when you first came to Arendal?'

'It was very like it is now, Anna, but the house wasn't as good. We had an open shed for a bathroom on the river bank and no chip heater. We had the verandas gauzed in but we didn't have the blinds, so you couldn't sleep out there. We didn't have much furniture and there was very little garden. We didn't have the front lawn, we didn't have the privet hedge around it, we didn't have the orchard, we didn't have the flower beds and the vegetable garden. Your father worked very hard in the early years to make it a pleasant place to live and to grow food for us.'

'Will he come back?

'No, Anna, he's not coming back. But we still have our house, we still have the river, we still have the paddocks and the sheep and we can still make our place better. It's our place.'

I get up and walk over to the fence to see if anyone is coming. Nothing, no movement on the horizon, only a shimmer of light dancing above the ground, a mirage of water. The boundary rider's family have probably gone away because it's too hard to live here. Dad is far away, who knows where. He'll never know what it's like for us here, he doesn't care. David's in the city; he doesn't know how hard it is for us or he'd come home and help Mum. The boys are at school and there's nothing they can do. There's no one to help us. We could die here of thirst and hunger and no one would know.

I walk back and flop down again on the chair next to Mum. I look at the lemonade bottle for a while then open it and smell it. I moisten my fingertip and taste it. It is flat lemonade. I take a few gulps and offer the bottle to Mum but she shakes her head.

'The only worse conditions I've seen than this are those the fettlers' wives used to live in when I first came to Arendal,' she says. 'They lived there with young children, no garden, barely any trees, close to the railway line, waiting for the train to deliver their supplies each week, through the raging summer and the bleak winters, winds tearing across the plains, dust storms, flies…' She leans back in the chair. 'Whenever

I think our life is hard, I think of them and what they put up with, all for the paltry wages their husbands earned, a few shillings a week.'

She dozes while I wander around the yard. I hum to fill the silence and make up a story about a queen who lives in the desert in a far-away country and flies at night to softer places where it rains every evening and flowers and fruit grow wild.

As the sun drops down towards the edge of the earth, I wander down the track to see if anyone is coming. Near the horizon a small cloud of dust appears lit with orange light. Someone is coming. Maybe they can help us get the truck started so we can go home.

Women's work

Sometimes Mum talks as if I'm not here, with her eyes staring at some point beyond her. I listen but don't answer. I wish I weren't here.

'I can't understand what Henry sees in a woman like that. She's so common and she's ignorant. The only things she reads are cheap trash, women's magazines. I've seen her sitting on the back veranda at Wyalgie with curlers in her hair and bare feet, a cigarette hanging from her mouth, reading *True Confessions*. She dyes her hair – it's not naturally red.

'She drinks beer too and bets on the races. I caught a glimpse of her once when we went into town, sitting in the public bar at the hotel listening to the races. I knew Daddy was in there with her because he'd told me he had to see a man about selling some wethers. A woman should never be seen smoking or drinking in a public bar. It's so cheap. Or wearing clothes that show the curves of her body without a proper corset and brassière.

'How on earth he could give up all he has here, his children, this place, all we've worked so hard for… I think he has no idea of what he's lost and he will live to regret it to his dying day.

'I'll keep this place going. He'll see what can be done with hard work and intelligence. I want Simon to be able to carry on here when he's ready. He's the only one who wants to go on the land. David wanted to come home and help me run it, but I said, "Certainly not! You are going to finish your course and practise as a city lawyer!" As for Malcolm, he wants to be a doctor.

'It's really quite unfair that we should be working so hard to provide him with an income, not to mention her. But that's the way the law is. It always favours the man in these cases. When he left, he promised he'd sign the place over to me in return for me bringing up the children. But promises are cheap. I think he meant it at the time but she's probably persuaded him he should hang onto it. David thinks I've a good chance of being awarded the title when the divorce is settled. He is, after all, the deserter. I'm not so sure, but I can only hope.'

Mum pays a man to do the crutching and lamb marking and a team comes for the shearing, but mostly we get the work done as best we can. Every day, we do the rounds of the paddocks, check the sheep for fly strike, look for breaks in the fences, sweep the mud out of the water troughs and make sure the windmills are working.

When we check the troughs, they're half full of muddy sand again. The wind blows it across the plains and sometimes there are willy-willies, where the dust whirls round and round picking up more dust and rising up in a long column.

We have to muster the sheep for crutching. The dirty grey-brown flock trudges ahead of us, heads down, occasionally breaking into a trot or surging off to one side or the other when one of the dogs decides to stir them up. I walk slowly behind, my hat pulled down to shield my face from the sun. I trail a stick behind me, letting it bump over the tussocks of saltbush. My feet are throbbing, my head aches, my throat and nose are dry and thick with dust.

Mum is ahead using her stick as a support or waving it at the dogs. 'Get be'ind 'ere, Bluey! Way beyond, Bruiser!' She mimics the way Dad used to speak to them and they obey.

She turns to me, her face running with sweat. 'Come on, Anna! Help me get these sheep penned up so we can get home and put our feet up. I'm dying for a cup of tea.'

I force my feet to go faster and catch up with her.

'At least now your father's gone we can do things properly, make sure the animals are well looked after,' Mum says as she strides ahead. 'He just didn't care any more, he gave up. He let them get flyblown, and didn't make sure they had enough feed and clean water. We're better off without him, so are they.'

I wonder where he is. I wrote him some letters and sent them to the address Mum gave me but he didn't answer. He doesn't love us any more.

*

Autumn comes with colder nights and a few showers of rain. Fresh winter grass is starting to shoot in the paddocks and the rabbits are busy. They breed in such numbers they eat all the grass and edible plants, stripping paddocks bare. Around the homestead down near the bend, they live in underground cities and at dusk you can see them hopping around, brown, ginger, black, orange and white as well as grey. Before they went away to school, the boys used to trap and skin them so they could sell the skins in town for a few pence each. They'd make a slit round the neck and peel the fur back, showing the smooth, pink flesh with ripples of muscles and traces of veins. Mum said they were vermin but the dogs love them. Now there are so many of them trapping is useless.

Mum buys a larvacide gun. Next morning before dawn she shakes me out of bed. We climb into the Bedford and she thrusts a Thermos of tea and a parcel of sandwiches into my lap. The truck shudders as she urges it over deep ruts in the road. I'm shivering, and I hug my arms across my chest and try to sleep.

'Anna! Wake up! Get the shovel.'

I tumble out and get the spade from the back of the truck.

'When I put gas in the burrows, I need you to close the entrance with some dirt.'

Mum leaves the engine running and the truck lights shining on the warren, and points the gun down the first hole, then presses the handle and releases the gas. Stumbling over the burrows, I move into the triangle of light and shove a spadeful of dirt in front of the hole. Then another lot, to make sure. Then more holes, more squirts, more dirt. We circle the holes, filling them with poison, closing the doors so the little animals inside will choke to death.

Beyond, the edges of the sky flush with pale pink and a shimmery golden disc floats up from the straight blue-dark line of the horizon.

Mum turns off the lights and stops the engine. 'Time to stop,' she says, putting the larvacide gun in the back of the truck.

I throw in the spade and climb into the cabin. Mum uncorks the Thermos and pours the tea while I unwrap the sandwiches. Cold lamb and pickle, my favourite, but I'm not hungry. I sip the sweet black tea and think of the rabbits waking up in their dark burrows, twitching and struggling to breathe.

'You know, I wish the boys were here at times like this,' Mum says between swallows.

'Me too! I wonder if there are babies down there in the burrows.'

'Probably. They're always breeding. But it has to be done.' Mum sighs and pours another cup of tea.

'You know,' she says after a long silence, 'I'm happiest when I'm walking behind the sheep. I feel as though I've done this before.'

'What do you mean?'

'I know it sounds strange. I can't explain it. I get the same feeling when I read books about the ancient world. It's very familiar to me. As though I've herded goats in the hills of Greece, or wandered on the steppes of Asia, a nomad following grazing herds of sheep or goats or cattle. I've never had that familiar feeling in cities or towns. That I belong, that I've always done this sort of work, lived this sort of life. Nothing seems too hard when I'm living like this.'

She looks out at the paddocks, where the sun's rays light up patches of silver-grey mixed with new green. 'This is my home. I can't imagine any other now.'

It's my home too but it's not the same since Dad left. Mum and I have to do the outside work and when things break and we don't know how to fix them, I wish he'd never gone away. When I go to bed, Mum is on her own. She has no one to talk to but me most of the time and she gets lonely and worries a lot. I think she misses him still.

*

At night after we've had dinner and cleared up, Mum sits by the fire, kettle on the coals to make her last cup of tea for the day, and I go off to bed. Mum sits reading and dozing, waking and yawning – long loud sing-song yawns. The cedar tree scratches and taps on the tin roof. Rain begins to fall, lightly at first then louder, drumming on the roof and windowpanes, rushing down the drainpipes.

The drought breaks

The long drought breaks with good winter rains; wool prices soar to the highest they've ever been, a pound for a pound in weight, and Mum rejoices.

'At last we can pay the Rural Reconstruction Board off! Just think, it's 1948, a year since Daddy left, almost ten years since we had to take out that loan. We've done what everyone thought was impossible. And without him.' She sighs, and gazes into the fire.

'What's the Rural Reconstruction Board?' I ask.

The kettle is singing on the coals. Mum reaches up to the mantelpiece for the tea caddy. She puts a couple of heaped teaspoonfuls of coarse black tea leaves in the pot, then pours the steaming hot water in and puts the lid on. She sets the pot on the hearth to brew and leans back in the wicker chair.

'Before you were born, years of drought and the Depression wore us down, and the last straw was a giant dust storm that buried most of the flock. We had to sell what was left of the lambing flock to pay off our debt to a pastoral finance company in town. They were fine ewes. Daddy had bred them with good results, and the wool had brought a high price, for those days. We were left without any way of earning an income.'

She leans forward and pours strong black tea through the strainer sitting in her favourite cup. On it pink and blue sweet peas trail over silvery grey fern. It is Royal Albert, part of a set Simon and Malcolm and I emptied our piggy banks to buy for her a few Christmases ago. It is chipped on one side of the lip.

'It was a blow to him,' Mum goes on, 'and it gave him an excuse for not trying. He had tried, he'd managed to breed some good sheep in spite of all the setbacks, and it had all been taken away from him.' She sips from the cup and cradles it in her hands. Her knuckles are red, lumpy and criss-crossed with fine lines.

'Anyway, your Uncle Austin came to our rescue. He lobbied the Rural Reconstruction Board to loan us money for restocking, and so we were able to keep going. But this is the first time the place has been out of debt since we came here. In the early days, we were in debt to his father, and to the finance company. If only he had waited…' She drains the cup and fills it again.

Since Dad takes the income from the place and gives Mum an allowance, she sells a couple of bales of wool on the side to celebrate, and buys a few luxuries – a kerosene fridge, a new dinner set to replace the one Malcolm broke, a case of Sauternes so she can sip a glass or two after dinner. She even buys a couple of dresses for herself and for me. She makes most of my clothes. I remember one Christmas when Dad was still here and there must have been some money to spare. I woke at dawn on Christmas Day and saw the outline of a cot beside my bed. At first I thought a baby had come to live with us. I crept out of bed to feel what was in it, and found a doll, fully dressed, with eyes that opened and shut. Next to it was a bought dress in my size, yellow organdie with white flowers, and a printed ticket.

I didn't play with the doll much; I'd never had one before, and it meant nothing to me. I gave it away to a girl about my age who visited us once. Her father was a boundary rider and they didn't have a proper house or any toys. I preferred playing imaginary games with fairies and nature spirits, and making miniature gardens. I'd fill a bowl with wet dirt, and find pieces of moss from damp places to make a lawn. I used leafy twigs and flowers to make orchards and flower beds, and sticks tied together with dry grass for the fence. But always, the next day, the moss was dried up and the flowers and twigs wilted. So I'd start again, hoping that this time the plants might grow.

The dress was the most beautiful thing I'd ever seen. I called it my ticket dress and kept it long after I grew out of it. But I don't have it any more.

Accident

Spring holidays come and the boys are home. It has rained all night and most of the morning, but after lunch patches of blue sky appear in the woolly grey clouds. The ground is shiny red with big puddles lying in the hollows of the driveway. I'm riding my bike no-hands round the stretch that swings past the wood heap. Our new pup is chasing me. Suddenly he darts in front of me. I swerve and fall off into a puddle. I untangle myself from the bike and try to stand up but my right leg feels numb. I pull down my lisle stocking splattered with mud to have a look. There is a jagged tear in my thigh. The innards are oozing out, purply-pink grainy lumps of flesh and trickles of dark blood. There is a lump of bloody stuff stuck in the end of the handlebar. I scream and fall down again in the mud. Simon and Malcolm rush over and pick me up. They make a chair of their hands and carry me inside to Mum in the kitchen.

'Heaven's sakes! What on earth has happened?'

Simon starts to say something but a sob breaks out and he turns away rubbing his eyes, so it is left to Malcolm to explain.

After Mum has cleaned the wound and bound it up, she tells the boys to walk to the nearest neighbours for help. The Bedford broke down a few days ago. She props me up in the armchair in front of the fire with my leg on a stool, an eiderdown wrapped around me. She makes a pot of strong tea and toasts bread over the coals and hands me a thick slice dripping with butter and golden syrup. My favourite snack, but I'm not hungry.

Mum pours tea into the sweet pea cup and stirs in two spoonfuls of sugar and some cold water. 'Eat up your toast and drink your tea.'

I nibble at the toast and sip the tea, watching the flames flicker above the glowing logs. The clock ticks, Mum throws some more logs on the fire. I put the cup and plate down and snuggle under the quilt. My leg throbs under the bandage, but the warmth of the fire, the sweet tea, the cosy chair and blanket lull me and I drift off into a dream of this place when Dad was here, the orchard and garden were green and thriving and I had safe places to play and hide in.

I'm woken by the dogs barking and the sound of a car engine.

Mum bustles in. 'Here they are at last!'

The boys carry me out to Mr Baker's little Buick car. He helps them settle me on the back seat and Mum climbs in beside me. We set off to town, leaving the boys to hold the fort. As I lie, my head on Mum's lap, I think of Simon and his tears. I haven't seen him cry before except for that time when Dad thrashed him for throwing the turnips in the river. Maybe he does love me.

I think of times when he and Malcolm let me join in their games. Simon was Bill and Malcolm was Joe. I was their little sister Susie.

'Susie,' Bill said, 'Santa's coming tonight. You need to hang your stocking up. And you must say what you want to get for Christmas.'

'Well,' Susie said, 'I want a Bayko building set. So I can build a shiny new two-storey house for us all to live in, with red and white bricks and red roof and green windows and doors.'

'Now, Joe,' Bill said, 'You must say what you want.'

'I want a crystal radio kit. I want to make a radio so we can listen to serials at night when we're in bed. And Bill, you must say what you want.'

'I want a boat with an outboard motor so we can go down the river and catch lots of fish and explore the bends. Susie, you must ask if you can come with us.'

And so we'd go on a fishing trip down the river and have adventures till we got sleepy. After they went away to school and Mum moved me into her bedroom, they didn't play Bill and Joe any more and I didn't join in their games much.

I try to sleep but I need to wee. After we've got onto the main road, I whisper to Mum, who leans forward and murmurs in Mr Baker's ear, and he stops the car. I'm embarrassed that this skinny little man has to know.

He is the manager on the station to the west of us, but in Dad's book he's not a real man. 'Weedy little snob! He got the job of manager because his dad was a successful stud breeder, but he doesn't know the first thing about breeding sheep,' Dad scoffed.

When Mr Baker married his housekeeper, Dad laughed. 'Poor woman! Must've been short of men!'

Why isn't Dad here? Why do I have to wee in front of a stranger?

I struggle out of the car and squat awkwardly in soft dirt beside the road, one leg bent, hurt leg stretched out in front. Hot liquid runs down scalding my thighs. I start to cry. Mum helps me up and puts her arms round me and kisses me on the cheek.

'Mum,' I say between sobs, 'Why isn't Dad here? Why doesn't he write to me?'

'Darling, we've just got each other now. I'm sure Daddy still loves you but he probably feels guilty and doesn't know how to fix what happened. He has to make his own life now. He's chosen to leave us and we just have to accept that and make our lives without him. Some day he'll realise what he's lost.'

Fortunes

Mum and I have been watching the road all day. Mum is expecting a new utility to be delivered. David bought it in Sydney for us, and David's friend Tom, who's Mum's lawyer, is driving it to our place.

Towards late afternoon, I climb the cedar to keep watch. Trailing a cloud of dust, a vehicle of the right shape slows down and turns into the home paddock. I rush in to tell Mum, and she takes off her apron and smooths her hair. She walks out to the driveway, I run ahead. A lovely shiny grey Austin with smooth curving lines comes towards us. I run round to the driver's side as it pulls up; I stop with a jerk. The mudguard is crumpled and flakes of paint are lifting off. Tom climbs out and smiles at me, then turns to Mum.

'Mrs Anderson, here we are! Your new ute!' He points to the mudguard as Martha walks round to greet him. 'I'm sorry about the dint.' He puts an arm round me and kisses me on the cheek. He waves his other arm over the mudguard. 'I was trying it out to see how fast it would go, and hit a rut in the road. I lost control for a moment and hit a culvert. Damned shame, but it can be fixed.'

Tom is to sleep in Dad's room. He and Mum sit up late, yarning by the fire. I fall asleep to the murmur of their voices and dream that the Austin is new again, smooth and shiny all over.

Tom stays for a couple of days, and entertains us with stories of life in the city, things he and David do together, and some of the interesting cases he's had. His eyes are blue like Dad's but softer, and there are strong smile lines around his mouth. His wavy red-gold hair falls over his forehead. I love to hear him talk; his voice is soft and musical. He says he can read fortunes in people's palms.

Mum sniffs at the idea. 'I don't think I want to know the future!' she says.

I ask him to do mine.

'Hmm.' He frowns and runs his finger across my palm, then holds my fingers back to make the lines show up more. 'You'll have a very interesting life, lots of changes. You'll be lonely sometimes, but you'll be searching for something that is hard to find.'

'Will I be rich?'

'Sometimes you'll have plenty of money, and sometimes you'll have none.'

'Please tell me more. Where will I live? Will I marry? And have children?'

He gazes at me for a moment, then looks down at my palm. 'I can't tell you any more.' He closes my hand and squeezes it in his. 'Let it unfold. Just try to make the most of whatever happens.'

*

My big brother David is coming from Sydney on Christmas Eve with his fiancée, Jenny, to spend a couple of weeks. Vera's still in England studying to be an actress. Before David and Jenny arrive, Mum decides to take Malcolm and Simon and me to Griffith, about a hundred miles away, to shop for Christmas presents.

'Are you going to send Dad a card?' I ask the boys when we're planning what to get for Mum.

Malcolm looks at Simon. He's two years older, but you'd think Simon was the older one.

'Don't be silly!' Simon scoffs. 'We hate 'im. Don't we, Malcolm!'

Malcolm stares at the floor for a minute. 'Yeah…Mum says we're better off without 'im and I reckon she's right.'

The first Christmas Dad was away, I sent him a parcel with a pair of socks and some tobacco. And a card. I sent them to the address Mum gave me. I never got an answer. So I know he doesn't love me, he's never really loved me, and I'll never see him again. I've started to kill him in my heart.

*

We set off early in the morning and drive eastward, crossing over the river at Carrathool to travel along the main highway, which is in better condition than the one on our side of the river. We stop at Carrathool to have a cup of tea and a biscuit in the park by the river. The town is tiny, two shops and a handful of wooden cottages. Each house has a pitched tin roof, two windows shielded by blinds like eyes asleep, a chimney and a rainwater tank at one end. A few vines and weeds grow around the fence, and there is the usual dunny in the backyard. Mum is scathing about the town; she says the people who live here have loose morals.

She says that when she was teaching during the Depression, the first maid she had to look after David and Vera had gone to school at Carrathool, catching the train from the siding near her parents' farm in the morning and returning on the afternoon train. 'I had to get her parents to come and take her home. She turned out to be quite unsuitable. Then I was fortunate to get Rita, who was worth her weight in gold.'

'Why did you send her home, Mum? What was wrong with her?' I ask.

We're sitting under the shade of a large river gum sipping our tea. The sleepy green river slides past so slowly you can only tell it is moving if you watch a ripple of current or a leaf floating on the surface. Simon and Malcolm are shying gumnuts across the surface of the water.

Mum pours herself another cup of tea. 'She fell pregnant. She seemed a nice enough young girl, but I think her schoolmates had been a bad influence. One of the fettler's wives told me revolting stories about what the boys and girls used to get up to on the train.'

'What did they do?' I think of the shabby brown leather seats, the narrow corridors, the stink of diesel fumes in the noisy little two-carriage train, and I try to imagine the bodies of girls and boys wrapped together. Did they have intercourse? If so, where did they do it?

'We won't go into that! I didn't know about it when I asked Edna to come and look after David and Vera. She made friends with another maid. I discovered later *she*'d had two illegitimate babies, both adopted before she left hospital! Towards the end of the year, a circus came to town. One night, Edna went out with the other girl, and didn't come back until after midnight. I waited up for her. I questioned her, and she admitted that she and her friend had been with two boys from the circus. I wrote to her mother, and she came in at the weekend to take her home.'

'Did she get into trouble?' I pull another buttered Sao biscuit with cheese from the tin.

'Yes. Poor young thing!' Mum sighs and stares into her cup.

'What happened?'

'She died a horrible death. What came out at the inquest was that her father had bought some arsenic. When he came home, he put it on a shelf, and pointed it out to her. He said he warned her not to touch it. She did, poor girl. The inquest was reported in full in *The Riverine Grazier*. It was just before school went back. You can imagine how we felt!'

As we drive on from Carrathool, I think about a young girl dying from poison because she is pregnant. Why is it so terrible to be going to have a baby? Did her father really make her die?

*

Christmas dinner will be ready late, after the presents and the clearing up. I've peeled the vegies and set the table, and the boys have chopped the wood and swept the floors. David and Jenny are up at last, so we can open the presents.

After we've cleared up, David grabs Jenny's hand and says, 'Let's go for a swim. You don't know what swimming is until you've done it in the Murrumbidgee!'

'Is it sandy? I don't like muddy bottoms!' Jenny looks doubtful.

'Of course it's sandy. And the water is cool and sweet.'

Below the windmill, the river is still deep, and there is a sandbank in the middle. Jenny stands on the bank holding her towel around her, looking uncertain, wriggling her toes in the sandy soil at the foot of the bank.

David is treading water a few feet out. He throws his head back and laughs. 'Come on! It's beautiful!'

He holds out his arms, and she launches herself from the bank and swims to him. They kiss, and he turns and swims to the sandbank with her following. I dog-paddle after them and the boys dive-bomb off the bank into the deep part.

I wish he'd come home to live. He would help Mum run the place and she would tell him her worries and he would fix things when they're broken and do the hard work we can't do. And he would read to me at night like he used to and play games with me sometimes. My big jolly brother. He's fun like Dad was but he doesn't have such a bad temper as Dad. And Mum looks up to him and listens to him and she doesn't nag him like she used to Dad. But he wasn't here when Dad left and he doesn't know what it's like to be the only one here with Mum. I'm just his little kid sister and he has eyes only for Jenny.

*

At the table, David opens a bottle of chilled Sauternes for the adults and Schweppes soft drinks for us, as well as the usual home-made hop and ginger beer. Martha brings the roast turkey to the table, shining golden brown, gleaming with fatty juices.

'Rally rally round the table! Fill yer bellies while yer able!' shouts Simon, first to sit down.

'Twofoursixeight! Bog in don't wait!' says Malcolm, rubbing his stomach.

Jenny smiles at me as she pulls her chair back and sits on the other side of the table from the boys. She is pretty, with wavy golden-brown hair and big grey-green eyes. Mum likes her.

'You can tell she's been brought up well,' she said to me in the kitchen when I was helping dish up the vegies. 'Nice manners, and a lovely clear voice, with rounded vowels and no dropped consonants. I'd like you to go to a school like she did, where young ladies can have a well-rounded education and learn some of the finer arts of living.'

There are two huge dishes of vegetables piled up high and a jug of rich brown gravy. After the turkey there is trifle with little silver charms hidden in it and ice cream. Now we've got a kerosene fridge, Mum makes ice cream every day in the summer. Now and then something goes wrong and all the food tastes of kerosene. But it's much better than the Coolgardie safe and eating salted meat most of the time. Once, Dad brought a big ice block home from town, and we were able to keep things cool for a while until it melted.

When Mum passes the pudding round, David gets the silver spoon and Malcolm gets the moneybags. I want the wedding bells but Jenny gets them. Mine is an anchor. Perhaps I'll travel a lot. Mum and Simon don't get anything. Mum is not fussed but Simon shoots dark looks at everyone and asks for another slice of pudding.

Plates are scraped and licked clean (we're allowed to lick them in the kitchen, not at the table) and the leftovers are covered and put away in the fridge. After the washing-up is done, Mum retires to her canvas chair and we go off to lie on our beds and snooze in the afternoon heat. This is a holiday; once the meal is over, no one has to do anything they don't want to.

Bobby

When Mum and I go into Hay, we always visit Great-Aunt Betty, who lives on the edge of town. She is in her eighties, and lives with two of her daughters. One of them has never married, and the other is divorced.

Mum says the divorced aunt's husband had been a gambler and a womaniser. 'He was worse than Daddy!'

I wish she wouldn't call him Daddy. He's not any more. I never called him that anyway.

'Have you heard anything from Henry, Martha?' Aunt Betty asks as her needle flies in and out of the satin-stitched roses she is embroidering on a tablecloth. They are shaded in many colours, with tendrils of bright green and darker stems.

'No, Aunt Betty, I haven't. My lawyer has negotiated a regular allowance, since Henry's taking the income from the property. I can't file for a divorce yet. It will be on grounds of desertion, of course, but I have to wait another two years. It's three years since he left.'

'My sister mollycoddled him, that was the problem,' Aunt Betty says, turning up the underside of her embroidery. 'He used to taunt his brothers till they'd turn on him, then run behind her skirts, and she'd shield him from them. Same thing if he got into trouble from his father. Henry would run to her, and she'd put her arms round him and tell George he was only little, he didn't know any better.' She cuts the thread, knots it close to the cloth and trims the ends, then chooses a twist of dark red from the pile of silks in her bag.

'She didn't let him play football at school because she said his heart had been affected by rheumatic fever.' She begins to fill in the bud at the end of the stem.

'Yes,' Mum says, lifting a piece of sponge cake onto her plate. 'I'm afraid he's never grown up. He loves nothing better than getting into an argument with someone.' She takes a bite of the cake.

'More tea?' Aunt Betty gestures to the pot.

'Yes, please! It always tastes better in a good thick silver pot like this,' Mum says, pouring herself another full cup. 'He was always the wronged party, as far as he was concerned. He gloated over his description of himself as the black sheep of the family, who was always straying from his pastures,' she continues, wiping her lips with the napkin. 'He's well and truly strayed this time.'

'You're better off without him, Martha.' Aunt Betty puts her embroidery down and takes a sip of tea and a bite of cake.

'I agree,' Mum says. Her eyes go watery, and she looks down at her cup.

I lean down to pat Bobby, the old cocker spaniel. He's sitting next to my chair, watching my plate, following my hand as I lift the cake to my lips. His tongue is bright pink and shiny, his eyes like saucers. He is black, fat and curly, with long ears that wrap round his nose. Aunt Betty says that's a sign of his breeding. His grandfather was grand champion at the Royal Easter Show. You'd never know, to look at him. He's like a little petrol drum on legs. I'd love to have him for a pet. I haven't had a pet since Curly.

I finish my second piece of cake, and lick the cream from around my lips. Bobby scoops up some crumbs I've dropped, and waddles out of the room.

'Tell me about when you were a child please, Aunt Betty,' I say, putting my plate on the table.

She picks up her embroidery again. 'We were always busy, but it was good to work hard and see the results of our efforts. Mother knew all the arts of preserving fruit and vegetables, curing meat, rendering fat to make soap and candles, sewing and needlework. Our kitchen was hung with bags of onions, bunches of herbs, flitches of bacon and hams. It was lined with bins. We kept flour and sugar in some of them.

We'd fill the others with cakes and pastries we made on baking days. We had a dairy, a cream-house, fowl runs, kitchen gardens, an orchard.' She rests her hands on her embroidery and leans back in her chair, gazing out the window.

'Mother and Father used to order household equipment in bulk from Anthony Hordern's catalogue three or four times a year. It was so exciting when the bullock tray arrived. It would be laden with supplies. Imagine it – there were baskets and barrels of goods, perhaps a clothes basket full of crockery, barrels full of sheets and other household linen.' She picks up her embroidery again and looks closely at the dark red rosebud.

'When I was small like you, Anna, the catalogue was my favourite picture book. It was big, thick, and every page was covered with small pictures of the goods in stock. Even farm implements, harness, tools, barrows, sulkies…'

Aunt Emmy, the younger daughter, comes in looking cross. 'Mother, that dog is impossible! Guess what he's done now?'

'What?' Aunt Betty sighs, putting down her embroidery.

'He's stolen the ham bone from the larder! I noticed it was gone and found him out on the back lawn with it.'

Aunt Betty looks at me, then at Mum. 'Do you want him, Martha? He's a darling, but he really is a bit of a nuisance to us. He's getting old and a bit deaf, and if he gets out the front gate, he just trots across the road without looking. One of these days, he'll get run over.'

I look at Mum, who nods and smiles back.

'Well, yes, I suppose we could take him. It would be nice for Anna to have a dog of her own, even if he is old. We've got a puppy, but he has to be trained as a sheep dog.'

I jump up and hug her, then Aunt Betty, and run outside to tell Bobby the news.

*

He sits on the front seat of the utility on the way home, next to the window, his nose pressed against the glass. When we reach home and I open the door, he jumps out and takes off, running round and round the garden, his stumpy tail wagging all the time.

Bobby takes to life on the land as if he is born for it. He loves chasing rabbits; he charges along at the rear of the other dogs, his ears flying back, his fat body wobbling from side to side. When they catch a rabbit, he lumbers up and grabs it from them, and they sit back, looking disgusted while he mauls it as if it is his catch. When we go out in the paddocks, he sits on the front seat beside me, while the sheep dogs hang over the sides of the back tray, panting and gazing ahead. They know he has special privileges they will never have, and they ignore him as much as they can.

At night in the winter, he lies on his side by the fire, his legs stretched out. He dreams, probably of catching rabbits, and his legs twitch; his lips puff in and out and muffled yelps come from his mouth. When he gets too hot, he struggles up and goes to the other side of the room, where he flops down till he cools off.

One day he disappears. We search everywhere for him, in all his favourite spots. I think that he's got stuck down a rabbit hole, like Winnie the Pooh, and will be able to get out when he's thinned down a bit. I look for him every day for a week.

Mum says someone may have seen him near the road and picked him up. 'They'll see he's a pedigree. They might take him home to breed from him.'

I don't think anyone would take him; he's too old and fat. Maybe he knew his time was come and went away to die.

It's part of life here. People go away and don't come back and sheep are killed so we can eat and pets grow up and get sold like Curly or they die or disappear. But I do miss Bobby. I miss him at night when we're sitting by the fire and I miss him when I get up in the mornings. I miss him when we go out in the utility and I miss him when the other dogs catch a rabbit and he's not here to pretend he caught it. We've only had him for a year, and I miss him so much. I even miss having to check his ears for cankers in the summer and comb the burrs out of his coat.

Neighbours

Summer has worn out its weary way and there have been good opening autumn showers, followed by heavy winter rains. The paddocks are lush green, studded with gold bachelor's buttons, white and yellow paper daisies and pink and mauve vetches. The river is running deep, and the trees are shining with new gold and red tips. Lambs frisk round their fat mothers, whose wool is thick and finely crimped.

It's shearing time. Mum gets in a team of four men. They sleep in the hut Dad built down near the bend and eat their meals at the house. Between helping Mum with meals and smokos, I work in the shed, sweeping up and picking the dags out of the fleeces. I love the smell of sheep, and the oily shiny floorboards.

The sheep are so patient as they sit there being shorn. When the shearer finishes, he gives them a push and they scramble up and out the hatch, shaking themselves and running off to join the others. These shearers are good; they don't make too many cuts and they finish the small flock in a couple of days. Dad would have been pleased.

The next task is dipping the sheep to kill lice and their eggs. We can't do this. We don't have the equipment, and it's too hard for a woman in her fifties and an eleven-year-old girl.

It's four years now since Dad left, and Mum and I have managed so far with help from the boys when they're home. But some jobs we need outside help with, or Mum has to pay someone to come and do it. Our neighbours on Wyalgie, two stations away, come to the rescue. The manager who employed Mrs Dalton as cook has gone, and Mum has become very friendly with the new manager and his wife. Mr Peterson asks her to drove the sheep to his paddock and stockyards near the railway siding where he and his men will do the job. In the yards, there is a special race with a pit in it; the men fill the pit with water and smelly milky chemicals and the sheep are forced to swim through it. We have to get the sheep there the night before, so the men can start early.

We set out in the morning with utility and dogs. Mum drives the ute on ahead a couple of hundred yards, then walks back and helps me and the dogs drove the sheep till we get past the ute. Then she does the same again. It's ten miles along the road and another two miles up to the sheep yards. Mum is doing double the distance, but when she gets tired, she sits in the ute and waits for me to catch up with the sheep. Or she lets me drive the ute ahead and walk back. The boys taught me to drive last holidays, and sometimes Mum lets me go on my own to the siding to pick up the mail. It's funny when I pass someone and they look twice to see who's driving the ute.

Weary trudging miles are our life now, doing men's work, following the sheep. Mum is content and does not complain.

As the sun is setting and the sheep are safely penned up, we call the dogs, climb into the utility and drive down to Wyalgie homestead.

Wyalgie is about fifty thousand acres, which isn't huge round here, though it is nearly ten times bigger than Arendal. It is owned by a pastoral company, like most of the big stations. The homestead is surrounded by sugar gums and willow trees. The drive leads you past a tall hedge and sweeps round in a circle in front of the house. Inside the circle is a thick lawn of buffalo grass with a central bed of standard roses enclosed in a low hedge of lavender. There is a tennis court between the house and the driveway. At the back of the house is a large vegetable garden. It's kept by a Chinese gardener, and Mum buys vegetables from him; we don't have time to keep up Dad's vegetable garden.

'Ah, missus, you got good stuff this week! Nice new spud, callot, pussnip, cabbidge, unyun – next week I give you more, pumkin maybe, beetloot. All lovely flesh stuff. Oney ten bob this week, velly cheap.'

He talks as he bends over the rows of carrots, pulling out the fat ones, shaking off the dirt and dropping them into the sugar bag. He never stands up straight, his back is curved like a bent spoon. He pulls a sharp knife from a sheath in his belt and cuts some leaves of silver beet. 'Here, I give you these for flee,' he says as he drops them in the open bag. He closes the bag with a bit of rope and hands it to me, grinning from under his floppy felt hat. 'Here, missy, nice callot for you', he says, pulling a small one out of the ground and rubbing the dirt off it on an edge of the sugar bag.

Outside the garden are sheds and a large pond with an island in the middle and a bridge across to it. The pond is home to many ducks and geese that nest on the island and keep the water green and slimy with their droppings. Mrs Peterson breeds turkeys too. They have dark shiny feathers and wrinkled red combs and the cocks make a weird gobbling noise. My favourites are the geese, big-bodied birds with white feathers dappled with grey. They waddle around in family groups, honking like a brass band out of tune when one of the dogs comes too close. Mrs Peterson feeds her poultry with special mash to get them fat.

> O-oh what have you got for dinner Mrs Bond?
> 'There's geese in the la-ar-der and du-ucks in the pond.
> Dilly Dilly Dilly Dilly come and be killed
> For you-u must be stu-uffed and my cu-ustomers filled!'

I walk over the bridge, shaded by big weeping willow trees, picking my way through the duck poo to the island. It has a little shelter built out of branches for the ducks and geese to sleep and nest in. I collect all the eggs I can find and take them in to the cook.

Next morning, after an early breakfast, we stand in the Petersons' sitting room near a crackling fire that smells strongly of gum leaves. The big tortoise-shell cat is curled up in the best armchair by the fire.

Mr Peterson stands in front of the fireplace with Mum. 'Great season, Mrs Anderson. You can expect a bumper price for your wool. Prices are higher than they've ever been, a pound a pound for fine wool.'

Mum always calls them Mr and Mrs Peterson, and expects them to do likewise, though she regards them as our best friends. She smiles at him and takes a deep breath. 'Ah yes, it's another wonderful season. Even better than the last one. When I think of all the years Henry and I went through – drought, the Depression, more drought – he gave up too soon.'

'You have to have a lot of faith to stay on the land out here, or a lot of capital behind you, a lot of acres. It's very hard for small farmers. It's a wonder you've survived this long. But you deserve the good times, you've been through so much.'

Mum nods, and pours herself another cup of tea from the large teapot on the trolley.

Edward, the older of the two Peterson boys, picks up the cat and plonks down with it on his lap. He is wearing drill trousers and riding boots ready for the day's drafting and dipping sheep. His blond hair hangs down over his eyes, which are the colour of deep-blue delphiniums. My favourite flower. He is going on fourteen. He is short like his father and has a husky voice just beginning to break. Normally at this time of year, he's away at boarding school. But he is at home recovering from an operation to his right eye, weakened by an accident when he was little.

The boys and I have been out with him and his dad kangaroo hunting a few times, sitting in the back of the station ute. I'm not allowed to hold the rifle or have a shot, so I just watch and listen. And driving back in the dark, I lie down on the pile of bags, as close as I can get to him, listening to his breathing. He chats with the boys and swaps stories about shooting rabbits and kangaroos, and I dream of holding his hand, snuggling up to him, letting him kiss me.

He is in love with his cousin Rosy, who comes to visit in the holidays. When she is there, they sit twined together, cheeks touching, and he winds her curls round his fingers. I wonder if they kiss when they are alone, if they go further. Mr and Mrs Peterson don't seem to mind them being so close. Rosy is sixteen, with curly dark brown hair, large satiny brown eyes with thick black lashes and an olive complexion that blushes to rosy brown in summer. Mum says she is a true beauty.

Mum is in awe of Mrs Peterson's family, which she says is part of the aristocracy of rural Australia, and often she gives whoever is listening a list of the names in their family tree. I wonder why. She never seems to feel her family was good enough even though there was an ancient Scottish king in it and an English lord. She talks much more about Dad's side of the family than her own.

*

'You can tell a true gentleman by his inheritance and his manners,' Mum lectures me. 'Common people will always be hoi polloi. No matter how much money they earn, they'll only ever be the nouveau riche. We may not be rich, but at least our breeding shows,' she often says. 'What will other people think?' is one of her favourite reproaches, even though the neighbours are so far away they can't see how we behave.

Once, I ask her if she believes there is a god.

She replies, 'Well, some people think so, but I don't. Not a personal god, anyhow. I'm not a churchgoer.'

Manners are her religion. Again and again, she reminds us of how we should behave, so we know the rules by heart.

Mum's liturgy
- Show duty, courtesy and respect for your elders.
- Don't touch your genitals.
- Don't lie.
- Hold your knife and fork correctly.
- Don't rest your elbows on the table.
- Don't speak with your mouth full.
- Don't slurp soup.
- Chew your food properly.
- You are allowed to lick your plate, but only in the kitchen, out of sight.

The boys are allowed to pour their tea into a saucer to cool it, but only when they are in a hurry to go out into the paddocks.

Men and boys are allowed to swear, but not in front of women and girls.

A woman who swears, smokes or drinks in hotels is unfeminine and common.

Women should not wear trousers, because they show the buttocks. Their bodies should be decently clad, not attracting attention; when they dress to go out, they should dress well, in becoming and modest clothing that is graceful and not flamboyant.

*

The big rug is rolled up in the sitting room at Wyalgie, the floor has been polished, and coloured streamers drape the walls. Mum has been teaching me how to waltz; she holds me stiffly with her arm stuck out like a board. She sat up late last night finishing the hem of my new dress. We chose the material together, lavender-blue marquisette. The pattern looks lovely, with a gathered skirt and a loose bodice of pin tucks with covered buttons, gathered in at the waist. Mum got Baxter's Drapery to send some material away to have the buttons made. But when I put the dress on and look in the mirror, I feel stupid. The skirt is too long and the bodice too big. Where my breasts are supposed to be there are just two pimples on a flat chest, and the tucks in the bodice sag over them down to my rounded stomach, which sticks out more than my chest.

Mum is wearing a new dress. The top is black lace with a taffeta under-bodice; on the shoulder is a spray of crimson rosebuds set off by dark green leaves. The skirt is black chiffon, hanging in graceful folds round her ankles. She is wearing rouge and lipstick, and she's lost a lot of weight since Dad left. She looks really pretty. She sits straight-backed, ankles neatly crossed, sipping Sauternes, chatting with the Petersons and Mr and Mrs Murray, the manager and his wife from Ulonga, about the years of drought and the Depression.

'Yes, they were hard times,' Mum says, 'but I remember the good things too.' She turns to Mr Murray. 'Your predecessor, Angus, was a demanding master, but he took his responsibilities seriously, and ran a tight ship. He took great pride in his stud rams. They were pampered like pets.'

Mr Murray grins and looks at his wife, who makes a face as if to say, 'He's not the only one!'

Mum takes a sip of Sauternes. 'I recall a story about his wife. She'd been away, as usual, for the summer. When she came back, the drought was still fierce, and a flock of the best rams were grazing on the lawn that surrounded the house.'

Mrs Murray shakes her head at her husband. 'Don't you ever dare do that, William! If you do, I'll be on the next train to Sydney.'

Mum laughs and continues, 'She brought an important guest with her, a woman from one of England's oldest families, who'd come to Australia for a holiday. The wife was so outraged by the sight of the rams on the lawn that she didn't speak to her husband for three days, and he was forced to stay away from the table and from their bedroom!'

Mrs Peterson chuckles. 'Oh…that reminds me of my Aunt Hetty. She and her husband stayed at the Australia Hotel every year during the sheep show. One evening, dressing for dinner after a day at the showground, Aunt Hetty searched high and low for her embroidered linen face-towel and special soap. At last she found them, indescribably filthy, in the waste-paper basket. She knew at once where the dirt came from, and showed the evidence to her husband. "Hetty!" he said, looking shamefaced, "that ram's face was dirty! I had to wash it!"'

They all laugh. Mum takes another sip of Sauternes, and turns to Mr Murray again. 'Henry's father told me that when Angus's father established Ulonga, he was asked about buying rams, and he said, "Na, na, we'll breed our ain!" And so he did, with great success.'

'Yes,' says the manager, 'He made a good choice, breeding plain-bodied merinos, not those fancy wrinkly things that were fashionable at the time!'

'Oh yes, "Ramboolies" they were called, weren't they?'

'That's right,' says Mr Murray. 'That was one name for them, from a town in France, Rambouillet, where they were first bred. The other was Vermonts, after the American state that developed the breed. They were supposed to produce more wool, because of all the wrinkles, but it wasn't so, and they were too hard to shear. And they attracted the flies something terrible.'

Mum nods and listens with interest while he goes on about the virtues of merino rams. Mrs Murray turns and chats to Mrs Peterson about the next event on the social calendar, a tennis party she is planning for the end of the holidays.

I wonder what Mum's life would be like if she'd married someone better off than Dad – someone who manages or owns a property like Ulonga or Wyalgie; if she had servants to clean, cook and wash; if she didn't need to worry about how to feed her children; if she was able to buy plenty of books and study the subjects she loves – Latin, Greek, history.

I wish we could entertain like this, have people for dances and tennis and swimming. And live in a big house with comfortable furniture, and a garden with a tennis court, and a boat for fishing and trips along the river. I like the way we live, it's comfortable and familiar, but I'd like to have a house we can be proud to invite people to. Mum is ashamed of our place and never invites the Petersons to visit, so she always gives them generous presents for Christmas and other occasions, because she feels obliged to them for all their hospitality. I wish we could live like the Petersons and the Murrays do.

But David went to the city and Dad went away and the boys went to school and it's just Mum and me. I want to live here forever but I want it to be different. I want to be happy again and not have to worry about how to do all the work and whether we can stay on. I want Mum to be happy and not have to work so hard.

The gramophone is playing a waltz and Edward is dancing with Rosy. Simon and Malcolm have disappeared to the back veranda, where some boys their age are playing table tennis. I dream that Edward will ask me to dance, whirling me across the floor in graceful steps. He will take me out to the side veranda to a spot that is hidden from the soft glow of the half moon by the bougainvillea. He will tell me that I've never looked so pretty before and he wants me to be his girlfriend. He will press his lips on mine, holding me close and sighing my name. And when I grow up he will ask me to marry him.

A good education

Mum says I will have to go away to boarding school next year like the boys because I'm getting behind, especially in maths. It's 1952, five years since Dad left, and it's my first year of high school. It's nearly the end of the year, and I've only done six months' work.

Last year, Simon came home at the beginning of the year to help Mum. She'd sent him to an agricultural college for high school because he wants to go on the land. He was there two years but he decided he didn't like it and told Mum he was coming home to help her run the place. When Simon makes up his mind about something, he won't listen to anyone. Mum doesn't shout at him like Dad would have or tell him not to argue like she does me.

'That's it, Mum,' he said. 'If you send me back, I'll run away.'

So she let him come home. He worked really hard all day and fixed a lot of things that were broken and got the irrigation going again. When he was home, he and Mum would talk about the state of the paddocks, the prospects for rain and the wool crop, and what jobs needed doing first. I got on with my lessons and didn't have to work so hard outside. And Mum was happier. It felt better having him there.

But she didn't let it stay like that.

'Simon,' she said, 'you're only fourteen. You're too young to take on all this responsibility. Anna and I can manage OK for another couple of years. You'll go jackerooing so you can learn more about different ways of farming. Then you can come back if you still want to and work this place.'

Simon gave in. He'd struck rock. Maybe he wanted to get away and try different places and ways of farming anyway.

So now it's just Mum and me again.

*

'You're like me, I'm afraid,' she said after I finished my lessons, two weeks late and with a couple of maths problems undone. 'You're good with words but not with figures! I can't help you with geometry and algebra and trigonometry. I'm OK with arithmetic, but that's all. You need proper tuition.'

'But Mum, how will you manage? You can't do all this work on your own.'

'Of course I can. The boys will come home in the holidays and do things I can't fix, like windmills and fences, and if I need to, I'll get a man to come in and do heavy work. We've managed so far, me in my fifties and you still a young child, with only occasional help, so I'm sure I can manage on my own for the next few years until Simon comes home and take over.'

'But Mum, I don't need to learn more maths. I can learn enough here at home with you. I can read books from the library and do my lessons. I'll work hard and make up the lessons I'm behind in.'

I'd read books about country girls who educated themselves at home, when boys had tutors or were sent away to school. I like that idea, just studying what I want to and not having to do maths and science. I'd read all the great novels and books about modern and ancient history and about geography and the different countries of the world. I could write my own stories and become a novelist. I wouldn't study Latin like Mum; it's boring. But I'd like to learn French.

'Nonsense. You've worked very hard to help me keep this place going and your education has suffered. You deserve better. And you'll have other girls your own age to play with.'

'But I like living here, and helping in the house and the paddocks. I don't need other girls to play with. I don't want to go!'

'It's settled, Anna. Don't argue with me. I've written away to several schools, and I'll choose the best one for you. Your father has to pay for your education. Let him pay for the best you can get. I wasn't able to make those choices for Vera and David. But Malcolm and Simon are getting the education that's suited to their abilities and you should too.'

'Why can't I go to hostel and high school in Hay like Vera and David did? Then at least I can see you when you come into town.'

'I want you to go to a girls-only school where you'll be mixing with children of our own class, not with all sorts. Where there's a good standard of morality and manners. I want you to have a good education. You will do very well with good teaching and you'll be able to go on to university.'

I think I would be happier if I could stay in Hay, close to the river and the lonely plains and skies.

Mum chooses a Church of England girls' boarding school on a farm. It's a branch of the school that David's wife Jenny went to. The booklet paints a glowing picture: 'Healthy climate in the fertile tablelands, a school following sound principles of education and morality, and a diet of fresh farm food grown on school lands.'

We go together by train to visit the school, a stately group of English-style buildings overlooking a lake, surrounded by rolling green pastures with wooded borders and blue-hazed mountains to the east. The headmistress, Miss Matthews, receives us in her apartment upstairs in the building near the lake. She seems a kind, motherly woman. Her hair is short and plainly cut, her cheeks red, her eyes a clear greeny-grey. Her most obvious feature is her bosom, which is large and well trussed, jutting out above her broad waist and hips.

She shows us round the main building in the school, striding a couple of paces ahead. The main house is approached by a sweeping gravel drive circling a moss-green lawn and luxuriant rose bushes. She shows us the dining room and chapel and the dormitories for the junior school. As we walk along a dormitory, a closed-in veranda with rows of beds lined up along the wall, she tells us of rumours that before she came to the school, boys from the Catholic preparatory school a couple of miles away used to come at night and climb up drainpipes and through windows to get into bed with the girls.

'Of course, nothing like that happens now!' she booms with a hearty smile. 'We've put a stop to that.'

We go on by train to Sydney, where we stay with David and Jenny, living in a cottage in Hurstville with their baby daughter. We shop at David Jones for uniform from the list the headmistress has given us.

> Three navy serge tunics
> six beige cambric blouses, short-sleeved
> six ditto long-sleeved
> one navy wool blazer
> one navy serge suit
> one gaberdine navy rain cape with hood
> four striped cambric tea dresses, choice of three colours
> two blue rayon Sunday dresses
> one navy felt boater hat, one cream straw ditto, one navy beret
> two pairs brown lace-up shoes
> one pair brown regulation court shoes
> six pairs beige lisle stockings
> six pairs beige socks
> six pairs cream briefs, ditto singlets
> three long-sleeved woollen cream spencers
> three ditto short-sleeved
> six pairs navy serge bloomers
> two pairs navy cotton gloves
> six pairs summer cotton pyjamas, six pairs winter flannel ditto
> one summer dressing gown, one winter ditto
> one pair summer slippers, one winter ditto.

I am measured and fitted with these strange severe garments that are delivered in cardboard boxes; some have to be ordered and will be sent to Arendal. I have never owned so many clothes before in my life. I am horrified at the cost, more than I've ever dreamed of being able to spend on clothes. But it's to turn me into a navy and beige parcel stamped with the school's crest. When we go home to Arendal, we spend many hours making non-uniform items like pyjamas and dressing gowns and sewing name tapes onto each garment by hand.

I wonder what my new life will be like. I have to leave Mum alone in the lonely house in the middle of nowhere with no one to talk to, no one to help her.

We don't have a comfortable or easy way of life here but I don't want to leave it. It is so much a part of me that I don't know how else to live. I'm used to being alone a lot, reading and thinking aloud while I go about my work in the paddocks or round the house. Mum regiments my life as much as she can, but she is so preoccupied with her own work load she gives me a lot of space. When she does talk to me, mostly she treats me like a grown-up. She doesn't lecture me as much as she used to and sometimes she'll ask my opinion about something. And she doesn't complain about Dad all the time like she used to. We hardly talk about him now unless she has to get her lawyer to talk to his lawyer about something. She still calls him Daddy, though. And she does complain that he only pays her an allowance for running the property and still takes all the profits. Maybe that's why she likes spending all that money on my school uniform, because he has to pay the bills for my schooling.

The day comes, and Mum sees me and my suitcases onto the motor train at the siding on the first leg of my journey to a new life. It feels more like being sent away to prison as I sit and wave to Mum, a small figure standing there alone on the platform, flat plains shimmering behind her in the hot February sun.

As the train rattles through the empty paddocks, I watch the line of trees curving along the river and wonder what my new life will be like.

School

School is a regimented, unreal world where you have to wear a uniform most of the time and sit in rows in the classroom and play sport and go to church on Sundays and chapel night and morning. Where you sleep in a bed in a row of beds on a veranda that's been closed in and have to get up at six a.m. and be dressed and have your bed made and dormitory tidy, ready for inspection by six-thirty, then down on the sportsfield for sports practice even on dark frosty mornings that bite into your bones.

Where the matron gives a list of girls whose beds aren't made properly or whose drawers are untidy to the mistress on duty in the dining room who reads out your name and marks you down for a detention. Where the boiled eggs are like half-set cement, with black rings around the yolk. Where toast is cold and often burnt and jam is thin with seeds and skins in it and there's no butter.

Where you practise holding your breath so you can pretend to faint and make yourself vomit up your breakfast and stick your hot water bottle under your arm and drink hot water and tell Matron you've got a fever so that she'll take your temperature and let you stay in bed until the doctor comes and says there's nothing wrong with you and Matron sends you back to class. Where you dream of running away at night and catching a train back to Hay.

Where you save your pocket money and gorge on sweets at the tuckshop because you're so hungry and the food is so awful. Where there are no men except for the farm manager and his son and the mistresses are young and unhappy and lonely or old and divorced or widowed or never married and unhappy and bad-tempered and lonely.

Where there are no boys allowed and you have to learn ballroom dancing and dance with girls at the annual ball.

Where you get a detention if your tunic hem is more than two inches above your knees and you have to wear thick navy serge bloomers over your undies and lisle stockings in winter and blouses buttoned to the neck with the school tie tied correctly. Where one of the most wicked things you can do is tuck up your tunic into your bloomer legs and sit behind the dormitory wing to get your legs brown at lunchtime and sing pop songs.

Where you line up for assembly and say a prayer and sing the school song and listen to Plop list all the things 'you girls' have been doing wrong and deliver new sets of rules and punishments. Where you dream up new ways of making Plop disappointed so she will give more lectures at assembly and make more rules you and your friends can find ways of breaking.

Months pass in a dreary routine. I miss the place so much. I am used to an outside world where there is work to do to stay alive and to keep the creatures that depend on us and that we depend on alive. To sharing Mum's worries and plans and feeling a part of the rhythms of the days and nights and the seasons. I liked just having Mum to talk to and making up stories in my head.

I'm not popular. I'm bad at sport and good at lessons. I can't run fast, I can't hit a moving ball unless by accident and I can't do headstands and handstands and cartwheels or vault over the wooden horse. I wait in line dreading the moment when I have to run up to it, fearing the clumsy fall as I land behind instead of in front. I hate the early winter mornings at hockey practice on the sports field. The grass crackles under my feet, the chilblains on my toes and fingers throb, wind whips at my face. When teams are chosen, I am one of the last to be called.

I make friends with another new girl called Barbara. She is an Anglican minister's daughter. She wears thick glasses and her hair is cut short and plain and she speaks like a grown-up. No one else likes her.

She is homesick too. After school, we sit in the sunken garden, talk about our homes and cry and cry. Barbara's parents send her a parcel of lollies and cake, and she shares it with me. She gets me to go to Crusader meetings with her and pray with her in the chapel. I decide to get christened and confirmed, and Mum sends me money to pay for a white veil and a white prayer book that has a certificate glued in the front signed by the minister and the teacher I've asked to be my godmother. It says I know my catechism and am now a confirmed member of the Anglican Church. My godmother is Miss Hall. She is tall and shy with golden hair. She teaches history and is quite stern and reserved but I think she is beautiful.

I pray every evening that Jesus will enter my life and transform it but I don't feel any change.

*

When I go home for the holidays, the house is tiny and bare, cold in winter and hot in summer. The bush and paddocks are monotonous and empty. Mum's face has more lines and creases on it and her hair has lost its gold tints and faded to a dirty sort of beige with salt and pepper streaks. She's had it cut short and permed. It is frizzy and hard.

'Oh, I got sick of brushing it and tying it back,' she says. 'This is much easier to look after and it's more modern.'

This place doesn't feel the same as it used to. My favourite dog Bluey, the old border collie, is dead, and Nicky the pony had to be put down because he tried to jump a fence and got his leg caught in the barbed wire and it turned to gangrene.

Mum seems older and tireder. She doesn't seem as happy doing the outside work as she did before. It's as though she's doing things by habit, not because she wants to do them. She's absent-minded and when I ask her a question sometimes she doesn't answer me.

This holidays Simon isn't home because he's jackerooing. Malcolm's supposed to come home but when we go to the siding to meet the train he isn't on it. Mum stands there staring into the carriages until the train pulls out. She's still staring at the rails after it's gone.

'Mum, come on.'

'I wonder where he is? He wrote and said he'd be on this train.' Mum turns away and wipes her eyes. 'Come on, Anna,' she snaps, 'we'll have to go to the Petersons and I'll phone the school.'

We walk to the utility and she opens the door. 'My favourite child!' she mutters.

Bloody Mum! I always knew she loved Malcolm best after David. But I'm the one who's been with her all these years since Dad left. I'm the one who's listened to all her worries and her tirades about Dad. I'm the one who's helped her the most.

When she phones the school, they say Malcolm missed the train and would be coming on the next one at the end of the week. Mum's in a bad mood for the rest of the day.

I'll be glad to go back to school.

*

In second term, Barbara and I don't spend much time together any more and I drop out of Crusaders and give up praying to Jesus. I make friends with a couple of other girls in my class. One of them is Sally, nicknamed Salty. She has short curly hair, very white skin with lots of freckles and a trim figure with small breasts that stick out.

Salty has been here since she was eight, when her father died and her mother had to go out to work. She is average at lessons and good at hockey and tennis. She teaches me how to break the rules and get away with it. Her best friend, Denise, is from Broken Hill. Her mother works in a hotel, and her father is a boundary rider on the border of New South Wales and South Australia. Her nickname is Dingo. She only goes home for the Christmas holidays; other times she goes to Salty's place. She is little, smaller than me and thin with a pale face and a jutting chin. She has a long ponytail that she tosses when she talks. Which is not that often. No one teases her because she's tough and has been known to fight girls and win, and she gets away with lots behind the teachers' backs.

Mum sends me some money to buy a second-hand bike from a girl who's grown out of it, and at weekends me and Salty and Dingo ride on the roads around the farm. It is very hilly and I bring up the rear puffing. My legs ache as I push the pedals around.

Mum pays for me to have horse riding lessons, because I never learned to ride at home. Dad and the boys were too busy to teach me, or they didn't have a suitable horse, or maybe they thought I was just a girl and I didn't need to ride a horse. The riding school is near the old church at Bong Bong, a couple of miles from the school. Mum orders a pair of jodhpurs for me, which have to be altered for my short legs. I like the smell of the horses, the faded leather and sweaty smell of the saddles and the gloss of my horse's coat when I groom him. He is a chestnut pony, with his own idea of what a riding lesson is about. He doesn't respond to my urgings to trot faster, or break into a canter. We muddle along and I dream of becoming a star rider and winning blue ribbons at the show.

I audition for the choir, and get a part as an alto. The choir mistress teaches us the school song – 'winds of these uplands blowing, unseen by felt by all…' and some songs by Borodin and Debussy. One part of church and chapel I enjoy is the singing and the chanting of the liturgy. I love the rhythms and the tunes. The rituals and the music may not carry me closer to God, but they soothe my longing for a world where you don't need to wear a uniform, and the sky and open spaces surround you, and your imagination can lift you above the earth and carry you into another reality.

I even get a part in the school play, *Toad of Toad Hall*. I play Mole, a small timid animal. I go to Sydney on the train at Easter time and stay with David and Jenny, and Jenny gets me a grey T-shirt and tights and makes a furry cap with ears and a tail by stuffing a long grey stocking with toilet paper. The drama mistress sticks whiskers on my face and paints dark circles around my eyes. I make my entrance on stage popping up from behind a grass-painted cardboard bank chanting 'Scrape and scratch and scrabble and scrooge, scrooge and scrape and scrabble and scratch. Up we go, up we go… Pop!' With Ratty, I sing 'all along the backwater, through the rushes tall, ducks are a-dabbling, up tails all…'

All these things are supposed to make me into a well-educated, accomplished young lady. I try to learn the rules and fit in, but I am out of step. I'm too short, too slow, too plain, too brainy, too quiet. The only thing I'm good at is lessons, and that is not popular.

At least I'm not a weirdo. Josephine has greasy hair and wears clothes that are too big for her and smells of wet pants. No one talks to her. And Patience; no one minds her, but she is a bit strange. When she talks, she doesn't look at you, and her words come out in stops and starts. She looks like a stick and walks with a shuffle, and sometimes she just stands gazing into space. She is good at maths, though.

The prettiest girl in the class is Ruth. Her hair is golden brown, and she wears it in a high ponytail. Her skin is honey-coloured, and her legs are long and shapely. She is good at all sports and is captain of the junior hockey team. She calls me a beastly swot and gives me a hard time whenever she gets a chance.

Sunday night is cook's night off. Tea is salad – Spam and lettuce and tomato, followed by white bread and jam. At my table we compete to see how many slices of bread we can eat.

'I've had six,' I say, feeling a bit sick.

'Seven!' says the girl next to me, reaching for another slice.

The senior at the head of our table wins. She eats ten. She's a big girl with thick legs and a big bottom.

Down our end of the table, Salty leans across to me and whispers, 'She stores it all in her bottom half!'

I giggle and rub my stomach, which is hurting.

What a joke, calling it a farm school. None of the vegies or fruit we are given are grown on the farm. The meals are disgusting. The porridge in the mornings is thick and gluey with lumps in it and sometimes the milk tastes off. Lunch is usually some watery stew with carrots, potato and silver beet or slimy stinky cabbage or tinned peas. I hated peas at home. Simon called me a pea-dropper because I'd drop as many as I could on the floor. I eat them now; I eat everything, even the awful porridge. Most of us get our parents to send cakes and sweets, and we spend all our pocket money at the tuckshop. Sometimes Salty asks me and Dingo to go with her on a picnic when her mother visits. We go to some lovely valley in the hills, wade in the stream, cook sausages over a fire, and gobble tarts and cakes till we are stuffed.

We are only allowed to wear civvies on Saturdays and Sunday nights after chapel. During the holidays, I make a winter dress in the latest style. It is a knobbly wool mix with long sleeves, a waist and a straight skirt. The first chance I get, I put it on before teatime and go to the bathroom to look in the long mirror. But I've got fat again since I came back to school and I look like a sausage tied in the middle. Most of the other girls have nice dresses they wear at weekends in the evenings, shop-bought ones. Some of the girls have so many nice things, they wear a different dress every weekend. Once or twice a year, Mum buys me a dress or a jumper and skirt, but it is always her idea of what suits me best, of what is 'becoming' for a young girl my age.

During the week after our baths, we put on tea dresses, striped baggy things with a pin-tucked bodice and a white collar. When the laundry comes back in starched pressed piles, we have to collect it from the named boxes in the laundry room and put it away, and then after prep at night Miss Champion, the housemistress, calls out our names one by one to come and collect mending from her desk. We sit and work while she strolls around the room pointing out errors.

'Make your stitches smaller, Anna!'

'Sally, didn't your mother teach you how to darn? Here, I'll show you.'

Mum used to sit on the front veranda in the afternoon and weave her needle in and out of a sock stretched over a mushroom-shaped thing. I would sit nearby drawing on envelopes and newspaper wrappers that Mum had opened out and pressed with a warm iron to remove the creases. She tried to teach me how to darn but I can never do it as neatly as she did.

I don't do Art. I wish I could. The girls who do spend two afternoons a week in the art room, full of paint and paper and mess, and wear special smocks, covered in paint stains. I hear them calling out to each other, chatting and laughing as they work. Art is for the girls who aren't good at subjects like Latin and maths and French. In my intermediate year, Miss Matthews asks me if I want to learn Greek. So I have lessons after school. I learn the grammar and practise writing sentences as neatly as I can in curved script with elegant tails and rounded letters. We begin to read Thucydides' *History of the Peloponnesian War* in translation, and I practise writing some of the names in script. I love the way the words form long trails, like carved polished stones strung together.

In summer when we have swimming lessons in the lake, Salty and Dingo are out in the deep part practising lifesaving. Both of them can swim well.

'Dad taught me to swim in the dam at home,' Dingo says. 'You live by a river, Anna. You should be able to swim well by now.'

'I know, but I nearly drowned when I was little and I'm scared of putting my head under the water.'

'I'll show you,' Salty says, pulling me over to the side. She gets me to put my head in line with my arms, face down. 'Take a deep breath. Then put your head and shoulders under water, keep your eyes open and look straight down as you breathe out. Then roll to your side and turn your head at the same time so your mouth clears the water. Take another deep breath then roll back keeping your head in line with your arms and body.'

She gets me practising that for a while and then pulls me out to the deeper water so I can't stand up. 'Now start kicking your legs and keep that action I showed you.'

I try for a few strokes but I forget to roll my body and my bottom and legs sag down. I end up dog-paddling back to shallow water.

The teacher comes over. 'Good job, Sally. But now I need you to come and show the juniors how to save someone. Anna, come back to the shallows. I'll get you to practise kicking your legs properly. Then you can try the breathing like Sally showed you. Next week, I'll expect you to put them together.'

I long for the sandy riverbed at home and the clean green water swirling against my skin. Curling my toes in the slimy mud, I recoil from the clinging stalks of lilies and rushes.

*

In the winter if you leave clothes out on the line overnight, they're frozen stiff in the morning. You can flick them with your finger and they spin round the line. After morning chapel, you file into the classroom and before the teacher comes in you take turns to sit on the coil heaters to warm bottoms and fingers. In the evening, the bathroom fills with steam and girls' voices as you run hot mud-coloured baths and pile in two or three at a time. When you go downstairs, if the door to the basement is open, you can hear the boilers hissing and rumbling. Sometimes you wonder what will happen if one of them blows up.

Before Mum sent me away, she gave me some bras she'd made out of cotton with tucks and trimmed with broderie anglaise. Each one was a bit different from the others in size and shape, and all of them looked awkward when I tried them on, their empty spaces sagging over my tiny bumps. I stick them in my bottom drawer at school under all my underwear. When the other girls dress and undress, I sneak looks at their different-sized and shaped breasts and their pretty, shapely bras. I decide to save my pocket money and buy some proper ones when I need them.

Mum also sat me down on my little bed and explained about menstruation. 'Once a month, women bleed. It's nothing to worry about. Once your body starts to get ready for being a woman and having babies, the natural cycle is that the lining of the uterus starts to thicken, and an egg forms and is released. If it's not fertilised, the lining is released as blood.'

I shifted on the bed, remembering how I felt when she sat me on her knee and told me how babies are made. It didn't seem real to me and I hoped I wouldn't start bleeding when I was away from home. She gave me a packet of pads and a belt to hook them up to, but I've turned fourteen and nothing has happened.

'Oh, shit, Gert's come again,' someone yells from the toilet to whoever is listening. They complain about the blood, the pain.

Now, I wish I could bleed too. I am still a child and they know much more about life than I do.

On cold days after school, Dingo and Salty and I snuggle up together on the couch in the junior common room, cheek to cheek, arms entwined, reading the same book, *Gone With the Wind*, after seeing the movie at one of the Saturday-night film shows in the dining room.

We talk about having crushes. It's the done thing to have a crush on a senior girl.

Dingo says, 'That's silly, I reckon. Why have a crush on a girl when you can go for boys?'

'But Dingo,' Salty says, 'there are no boys here.'

'No,' Dingo replies, tossing her ponytail back, 'it's like a bloody nunnery. Some of the senior girls get changed into civvies under a culvert when they have town leave and meet boys at the cinema. I'm going to do that next year.'

Salty giggles. 'You'll get caught,' she says. 'Then you'll get expelled.'

'I don't care. I'll go home and get a job as a barmaid and do what I like.'

I think of Edward and his delphinium-blue eyes. 'I've got a boyfriend,' I lie. 'He lives on a big station near us.'

'Oh, how old is he? What's he like?' Salty says.

'He's three years older than me. He's going to be a station manager like his dad. He's got blond hair and delphinium-blue eyes, and a husky voice.'

Dingo leans closer. 'Has he kissed you? Tell us what you've done.'

So I tell a story about the dance at Wyalgie and how he took me out onto the veranda and kissed me and asked me to marry him when he grows up.

Dingo scoffs. 'I don't believe you. I don't think you've been kissed by a boy. I have. And more.'

'Oh, do tell, Dingo,' Salty says, giggling. 'What did you do?'

'We went down to the river and we did it.'

'What?' I ask. I think she might be telling the truth.

'He stroked my pussy and he got me to rub his dick and he came in my hand. I came too.'

Salty and I look at each other. Salty shrugs. 'Well, Dingo, you'd better be careful. Next thing you'll be going all the way and getting pregnant.'

The bell rings for hockey practice. As we walk down to the sports field, I think about Dingo and the boy stroking each other and wonder what it would be like to do that with Edward.

*

Salty gets a crush on the school captain. She sends her notes and collects things she has discarded, a ribbon from her hair or a hairpin that's fallen out, and is ball girl for her when she plays tennis matches. When you have a crush on someone, you want to be like her and you want her to like you. The glow she casts wears off on you and keeps you going between glimpses. Her looks, her popularity, her skill at hockey or running or softball, the way she walks, the things she says, the clothes she wears at weekends, the way she laughs. It takes you out of the mundane world of desks and classrooms and dormitories and rules and prayers and detentions and you dream of a different world where the rules don't matter and you can be who you choose to be and be with who you like.

In my third year, when I turn fifteen, I'm relieved to find I'm like the others after all. I have my first period, and get a crush on Pat. Pat is a fifth-year girl. She's captain of the hockey team and is tall, with long legs and short bobbed hair. After weeks of stealing glances at her in the chapel and at mealtimes and watching every hockey game she is in, I pluck up enough courage to send her a note, asking her if I can dance with her at the school ball. The ball is held once a year; no boys are allowed, we have to dance with each other and sometimes with the mistresses. From third year on, we have ballroom dancing lessons every weekend. Salty is very light on her feet and dances well, and coaches me in the waltz, the foxtrot and the Pride of Erin, but my feet don't always do what they are supposed to.

The night of the ball comes and I put on the dress Mum made for me. It's white muslin with a tied waist and a gathered skirt that falls halfway down my legs and puffed sleeves. It's old-fashioned, a bit like *Alice in Wonderland*. Salty's wearing a yellow taffeta dress with a full circle skirt that swirls out when she spins round. Dingo wears green to match her eyes, a cotton halter-neck with a full circle skirt. Her waist is tiny and her breasts are starting to swell so, although she's small, she looks older, maybe about sixteen. We sit and watch the seniors do the foxtrot. Pat is doing it with a girl who's shorter than her, so she's dancing the man's part. Her hips sway as she steps from side to side and her calves pulse above her slim ankles and high-heeled shoes.

Next dance is the waltz.

Dingo nudges me. 'Go on, Anna, it's time to claim your crush.'

I hunch my shoulders, then stand up and walk slowly over to Pat. She's talking to the girl next to her and doesn't notice me.

I stand in front of her and clear my throat. 'Will you dance this one with me?'

She blushes and smiles and stands up. She put her arm on my back and takes my right hand and stretches it out. We move off as the music starts and she guides me smoothly around the floor. Under my breath, I'm counting and hoping I don't trip or get out of step. We don't say anything. She looks over my shoulder and I keep my eyes focused on the crystal necklace she's wearing. I'm glad when the music stops.

That night in bed I wonder what it would be like to make love with a girl. What do they do? Do they just kiss and stroke each other? Pat has a nice mouth with wide lips that curl up at the ends.

*

On Sundays after church, we change out of uniform into dresses of blue rayon, the same pattern as the tea dresses. The rayon is soft, but it is starched at the laundry so that the folds hung in stiff creases. Every second week, we go to the little local church at Bong Bong on the hill. It is surrounded by big old fir trees. It was built of stone by convicts and the walls inside are plastered, with faded, peeling murals of the Holy Family and the disciples. There is an old pedal organ and one of the senior girls squeezes out the hymns on it. On alternate Sundays, we march two miles into town to the big Anglican church.

The minister is our Divinity teacher. No one likes him. He has a long nose that often has a drip on the end of it, and has eight children. In lessons, he tells us that sex is ordained by God for procreation, and is holy and beautiful between man and wife. He stretches out his legs as he sits on the teacher's desk, so we can see the yellow stain around his fly. We have to learn parts of the Old Testament by heart. In first term, it was the Book of the Kings, how David died after a reign of forty years, and then it was Solomon, the wisest of all, who built a temple covered in pure gold with two cherubim made of olive wood overlaid with gold, and all the walls of the temple were carved with cherubim and palm trees and flowers, and the floor was covered in gold.

I don't like the bloodthirsty parts, about people being beheaded and slain and animals sacrificed and their blood sprinkled on the altar. The minister sets questions about the deeds of the kings, and walks round the room while we write the answers. He pauses behind Jan, a tall girl with blonde hair and round breasts, and leans over her to read what she's written, brushing his cheek against her hair.

In second term, I make friends with a new girl, Carolyn, nicknamed Hicky. She is bright, and a fast runner. She is the ugliest girl in the class, with thick glasses over her bulgy eyes, a big frog-like mouth, and spotty skin. Her voice is gravelly, and when she laughs, you have to laugh too. She is often put in detention for answering back, for being messy and untidy, for not doing her homework.

This Sunday is a town day, so we wear our navy serge suits with long-sleeved blouses, lisle stockings, hats and gloves. Hicky and I have fun as we march along the dusty road. We make up rude names for the mistresses, and stories about their secret love lives.

'What about Plop?' I ask. Plop is our nickname for Miss Matthews.

'She's a lezzo,' Hicky says, with a throaty chuckle.

'Oh, Hicky, really! Who's her lover then?'

'Saggy-boobs. You know, that prefect who runs Crusaders. I've seen her going up to Plop's rooms at night after prep.'

'But they're so religious!'

'That's the type you have to watch! The "holier-than-thous"!'

On Sunday nights, lights out is earlier than usual, as there is no prep. Hicky is on the bottom bunk. We talk for a while, but the senior girl warns us to be quiet. I start to think about home, the river, the bends. I wonder what Mum is doing. She's probably made her last cup of tea for the night and is by the fire, yawning, making a mental list of the jobs she has to do the next day.

Hicky pushes her feet up into my mattress, bumping me up and down in the bed. She gets faster, and I roll off the edge of the mattress and land on the floor with a thud.

'Right! Carolyn and Anna! Come here!' The senior sends us to stand outside in the hallway at the foot of the stairs and wait for Plop to see us when she comes in.

'Hey, Plop won't be here for a while. Let's go down to the lake,' Hicky whispers.

'But, Hicky…it's cold out there!'

'Nah. Not if we run.'

She pulls me out the door and we skirt round the house in the shadows. The moon is up, and the night is still. We run down the hill, Hicky streaking ahead. She opens the wooden gate. The water ripples in the moonlight. It is very quiet, just a few frogs croaking.

'Let's go in,' she says when I catch up.

'Hicky, you're crazy. It'll be freezing!'

Hicky strips off her pyjamas and wades out to where she can't stand, then starts to breaststroke towards the reedy island in the middle of the lake. 'Come on!' She yells. 'It's gorgeous!'

Slowly, I pull my pyjamas off and take a few steps into the water. It isn't as cold as I expected, but the bottom of the lake feels slimy and wriggly, and I wonder what might be down there – eels, turtles, even snakes? I wish I were home with Mum, snug in my little bed, listening to her yawns.

*

'Miss Matthews wants to see Anna Anderson please, miss.'

I stuff the book I am reading into the desk and leave the room, wondering what I have done wrong. The head's voice calls out to come in when I knock on the door of her office.

'Yes, Miss Matthews?'

There is a woman sitting with her back to me, a familiar back. She turns around. It is Mum, pale and serious.

'Mum! What are you doing here?'

'Well, darling, it's a long story, but I've had to leave Arendal.'

'Your mother's had rather a shock, Anna. I'll leave you two alone for a while.'

Miss Matthews goes out, and I sit on the other chair, my eyes fixed on Mum's face, my heart beating nineteen to the dozen.

Mum sits looking at her hands, then lifts her eyes. They are empty, like the horizon at home. 'Your father came back.'

'Oh, when?' My heart thumps. 'Is he going to stay?'

'I'm not sure, but we can't go back there any more. I've left for good.' She gestures towards two suitcases standing near the door.

'What happened? What did he say?'

'I can't remember. But he made it clear he'd come to take over the place again.'

'What did you do?'

'He offered to drive me in the utility to the Petersons' place. So I stayed there until I caught the train.'

'What about our things?'

'I had no way of packing them. I'm sorry. I just had to get away as quickly as I could.'

I think of my collection of china animals that I'd bought with my pocket money, my books, the photo album with pictures of Dad and me and my brothers... 'But, Mum...what will we do? Where will we live?'

'I don't know, darling. We'll manage somehow. I'm on my way to Wollongong to stay with Irene for a while, and I'll look for a teaching post in the city. But I wanted to come and see you first, to tell you what's happened.'

'But...Mum...what about Dad? Does he want to live with us again?'

'Apparently not. He didn't try to persuade me to stay. I think he wants to sell the farm. In any case, I wouldn't have him back.'

Next day at the train station, Mum's mouth is set in a firm line and her forehead is deeply creased. 'Be good, Anna. Miss Matthews is concerned about you. She tells me you're friendly with a girl who's a bit of a troublemaker. She said you were both caught swimming in the lake recently, after lights out on a Sunday. You should know better. Don't let me down. You'll be dux of the school if you work hard. And don't worry...I'll find somewhere for us to live.' She kisses me on the cheek and moves towards the train. The feather in her hat shivers as she climbs into the carriage.

Homeless

Aunt Irene lived alone until she was in her fifties, when she married a big, jolly Welshman who sang in the church choir. He had been a miner in Wales, but in Wollongong he worked on the railways, something to do with the freight trains that carried coal from the mines at Port Kembla. The first time I went down to Sydney on the train to visit Aunt Irene on my own, they met me at Central Station. It was after Dad left; I was probably about eight. Mum made sure I had a sleeper, but I hardly slept all night, and by the time we got to Central, I was so nervous I'd bitten all my nails down to the quick.

Aunt gave me a peck on the cheek, and a big, burly man with a smiley face held out his arms. I let myself be folded into a bear hug, an earthy, coal-smelly one, and I burst into tears, so he carried me out to where we collected my luggage and caught the train to Wollongong. I loved him. I called him Uncle Bill. He had thick silver hair. Sometimes when I sat on his knee, he let me twist some of his hair into tiny plaits and tie them with blue ribbons. When he and Aunt went out at night to choir practice or some other function, they took me in to sleep in the old aunties' house next door, in the little front sleepout. When they came in to fetch me, I would pretend to be asleep, and Uncle Bill would pick me up and carry me home on his shoulder. I would breathe in the tweedy smell of his jacket and the musty, dusty coal smell underneath it.

I slept in the divan bed in the sitting room, listening to Aunt giggling in the bedroom. Mum never giggled. Come to that, I'd never heard Aunt Irene giggle before either. She sounded like a little girl. I longed to ask her if she was going to have a baby. But I thought she was probably too old.

When I was in my first year at boarding school, Uncle Bill died of lung disease. After his death, Aunt threw herself more than ever into rescuing stray cats. She couldn't bring them all home to live with her but she got up early every morning and drove round all the parts of the city where they lived, leaving meat and milk for them.

Now in school holidays I go on the short train trip through the tablelands to Wollongong, where I sleep next door at the old aunties'. Mum sleeps on the divan in the living room. My bedroom smells musty, but I like the small iron bedstead with its lace cover, and the yellowing cotton lace curtains with holes that aren't supposed to be there. There is a mat beside the bed with roses on it, and a china chamber pot that I empty in the outside dunny in the mornings, stepping with care on the uneven bricks slicked with moss.

The garden is tangled and overgrown, with thickets of little cream and pink roses that ramble over the other bushes and across the pathway, and dark tangled masses of vines reaching for the light. There is an apple tree, gnarled branches clad in grey-green lichen, and stems criss-crossing and lacing together. There are a few little apples hiding among the leaves, but they don't get ripe, just stay green, then shrivel up. The best thing is down the bottom of the garden, an old well with a round brick wall and a cover of old boards. There is a round hole in the cover, and if you throw a stone down you can hear it splash.

The bedroom has its own entrance, and I see little of Aunty Sue. Her sister Bay died a couple of years ago, and Sue is in her nineties. She lives like a ghost, creeping from room to cluttered room and eating little of the food Irene cooks for her. She is alone and frail, a shrunken little Victorian lady still dressed in long dark skirts and blouses with long sleeves and high collars, surrounded by furniture from a past age and photographs of her family. She thinks I am one of her sisters as a child.

Mum makes several trips to Sydney to see her lawyer about a divorce from Dad. She says he is living with Mrs Dalton somewhere interstate and has put Arendal on the market. She hopes for a financial settlement giving her at least a half share of the sale price. She registers with the Department of Education again, and takes a job in a western suburb of Sydney when I return to school for second term.

Irene catches cold from doing cat rounds in the wet weather and it gets onto her lungs so she has to go to hospital. She dies in the sanatorium before the end of the year.

My first experience of seeing a dead person is when I see her laid out in the coffin wearing one of the jumpers she'd knitted, ribbed in lavender blue with a band of raised bobbles and purple and white flowers trailing across her chest. Her hands, pale and bony, are crossed over her stomach. But her fingernails are painted pale pink and reflect the light shining from the lamp over her coffin. Her grey-brown hair is shiny, tightly curled and waved. Her cheeks are pink and her lips are red, folded in a tight line. There are a couple of frown lines above her nose. I wait for her to unfold her hands, open her eyes, reach her hand up to pat her curls and look at us accusingly, asking about her cats, whether they've been fed, who will look after them.

We drive in the funeral car through the mountains to Sutherland cemetery, where she is to be cremated. I don't know what to say or how to act. Mum looks severe and sad in a grey tweed suit and a grey felt hat with a single black feather.

The seven cats that shared the house are put down.

Mum comes to teach at my school. She teaches senior Latin and my favourite subject, English. So now I am not only a beastly swot – I am the teacher's pet.

Of study and sex

Mum is at my school for nearly three years.

English is my best subject, and I always get top marks for it, even when I try not to. Mum is a dedicated teacher, and an exacting one. She puts an enormous amount of work into her lessons and her marking, and she returns our written work with lots of detailed comments in her delicate writing in red ink in the margins. Those girls who don't try or are not good at English have a lot more writing on theirs, or sometimes just a comment: 'See me after the lesson!'

One time after she's dressed down the ones who've failed the exam, Frieda, an outspoken girl from a rich Jewish family, says to me, 'Anna, you poor sucker! I've never seen a woman smile so sweetly and have such poison coming out of her mouth as your mother!'

Mum has a gift for chastising wrongdoers in polite, perfectly constructed sentences, using long words that some girls don't understand; but the tone and the way she looks at the offender makes them feel belittled and ashamed.

I visit her in her room. As a senior girl, a fourth year, I live in The Cottage and she is the housemistress there. We talk for a while, and she gives me fruit or cake she's saved from the meal at the high table; but I feel awkward, not myself; I pretend. I guess I've done that with her ever since I was little and I learned that she had high expectations of me. I resent the invisible barrier her presence puts between me and the other girls, but that barrier is between us too. Perhaps if I were a boy it might be different. From early childhood I became self-conscious and kept my self hidden as much as I could. The first time I developed this habit of secrecy in self-defence – like pretending I'd had a shower and brushed my teeth, hiding my bloomers if I wet them – I was very small. We were expecting visitors, and I was so excited I started to bite my nails. She scolded me for it, and after that I did it when she wasn't watching, as I did other things.

Having her at my school makes it more difficult for me to have a secret life behind the rules. The more rules adults make, the more things kids will do behind their backs. It's not just the fun of doing something forbidden, it's the fun of flouting authority. But I feel sorry for her, having to live here like a nun, with no home of her own, being unpopular with the girls, and I don't want to make her life harder by shaming her. Or to have her scolding me and telling me how I've disappointed her. So I stop climbing out the window at night after lights out, like we love to do when the apples are ripe in the orchard next to The Cottage. Despite the grubs in them, they are delicious, crisp sweet Jonathans; no bought apple ever tasted so good. I don't join in the midnight feasts any more, when the others hoard their tuckshop and gifts of cake and sweets their parents have sent, and creep down to the gym where they can make a noise. As for the forbidden picnics in the summertime in the Hundred Acre paddock, when we strip off and swim in the creek, picking off the leeches when we get out – I go a couple of times, but one time we get caught and I am carpeted by Plop, and Mum gives me a lecture about disgracing her and my pocket money is stopped for the rest of the term.

But I do other things she doesn't know about, sunbaking behind the gym with some of the others, our skirts pulled up round our waists and our bloomers tucked up round our crotches to expose as much of our legs as possible. And I sabotage my music lessons, stop practising, because I hate having to sit in the music teacher's pokey little room that smells of stale porridge and dog, while her pet pug lies snuffling and snoring in the armchair, and she sits beside me and slaps my hand when I play a wrong note. She tells Mum I have no musical ability and the lessons stop.

I go to the Head school in Sydney for the last term of fourth year and all of fifth year, because Mum and Miss Matthews agree my conduct and my work have deteriorated since she joined the staff. The Head school is a much happier place. And I don't have to worry about Mum any more. There are only sixty boarders here instead of four hundred, and as senior girls we have privileges like day leave and weekend leave. There are still lots of rules, and the emphasis is on character building not on academic achievement, but we don't have to play as much sport, and the food is good; on Sundays we get a proper roast dinner followed by ice cream and a second helping if we want.

I still feel as though I'm wearing a mask, wanting to be like the others, ordinary girls who laugh, play sport, misbehave, have nice clothes to wear, listen to pop music and have crushes. It is a culture where sport, looks and charisma are the currency of popularity, moral character is the model of the establishment, and academic achievement is somehow lost in the middle, although lip service is aid to it.

I'm not a beastly swot, but I do enjoy most of the subjects I take, and want to do well. So when final exams are approaching and I find the one-and-a-half hours' prep time we are allotted is not enough, I and some of my friends start setting the alarm for three a.m., and getting up to study in the senior boarders' sitting room. The matron springs us, and reports us to the principal. The others are given a group reprimand, but I am singled out. As I stand on the mat in front of the principal's desk, in that elegant study with the bay window overlooking the grounds, she peers at me over her half-rimmed glasses, and lectures me about setting a bad example to my friends.

'You should use your time better in the afternoons. You will be dux of the school, and you should be a role model. Our mission is not to turn out blue stockings, intellectuals, it is to bring girls to their maturity as well-rounded members of middle-class society.'

She strips me of my conduct badges, except for my prefect status, and tells me I have no hope of any conduct awards at the end of the year. If you can't be good, be clever, is the moral I take from this.

*

We are allowed to go out with boys on day leave in fifth year, if our parents give permission after they're told the name and address of the boy's family. My first boyfriend's name is John. He is polite and has pimples and wealthy parents with a big house in the eastern suburbs and an older brother with Down's syndrome. He comes to the school ball as my partner, and we dance awkwardly together, and don't steal outside like some of the others to kiss and cuddle under the trees.

My first real kiss happens in swot vac, when we're supposed to be studying for the Leaving Certificate exam.

Katie, one of the day girls, invites me and my friend Naomi for the weekend. 'You've gotta come. My parents are away, and I'm gonna have a party,' she says.

Ni and I think Katie is fast because she has a regular boyfriend and has told us she isn't a virgin. She disappears early in the evening with her boyfriend, and Ni and I drift outside. A couple of guys come over and start chatting us up. Roger is gorgeous; thick, wavy brown hair, dark brown eyes, and a throaty voice. After some flirting, he invites me to sit on his knee, and we kiss.

'I'd love to go further with you,' he says when we surface. 'But I can't. I've been a naughty boy and I have to be careful for a while.'

His mate laughs and they exchange knowing looks. Ni lifts an eyebrow and shakes her head at me. I think I know what he means. I'm wary, but I like him so much, I want to see him again.

Back at school, I wait in a fever for his phone call, which comes about a week later. Nothing much more happens while I'm at school because of the curfew. We start dating seriously in the Christmas holidays. He is the son of wealthy North Shore parents, and is taking a gap year before uni, driving a truck. He's knocked around, I know, and can get any girl he wants.

'I've got a sort of girlfriend, but it's not serious. It's just convenient for both of us. It's you I like best. I want you to be my girl.'

I am flattered he's chosen me, and I shiver every time I heard his voice. But a little voice tells me he isn't 'a suitable young man', as Mum would say; he is a sweet, sexy guy, certainly not interested in books and ideas. He is going to study accountancy, and his ambition is to make a lot of money and drive fast cars.

We go closer and closer each time we see each other. We pet on the back seat of his Holden at the drive-in and jive at parties to Little Richard and Buddy Holly. I sit on the floor with my full circle skirt and rope petticoat spread out while he fingers me. When we kiss outside my house, his warm body pushes hard against mine.

The last straw is a party at his house when his parents are away. Couples are taking it in turns to go into the bedroom. Roger is drunk, and wants me to go in with him. I make an excuse and find Ni and her boyfriend and ask them to take me home.

He rings me a few times after that but I let Mum answer the phone. She tells him I'm busy studying. She doesn't approve of him.

There are many others, but none are attractive or persuasive enough to tempt me to cross the line. Every time I go out with a boy, Mum sits up waiting for me, and when I come in, she cross-examines me and repeats her warnings.

'You have to be careful, Anna. Men want to take your virginity. Once they have, they will lose interest. You have such a wonderful opportunity, being at university on a scholarship. Don't throw it away. Sex should be kept for marriage. It has no value otherwise.'

Mum and I live in a one-bedroom flat on top of a house in Lane Cove. David and Jenny and their children live on the ground floor. So Mum and I share a bedroom, and I feel as watched over and ruled as I did at boarding school. I live in the shadows.

In my first year of Arts at Sydney Uni, I am a fringe-dweller. I don't join any of the student societies, and I sit on the edge of the circles that gather in Manning House coffee shop around stars like Clive James, Germaine Greer, Robert Hughes, John Bell, Ken Horler and Richard Neville. They are a few years older than me, and from a different planet. They are articulate, gifted, charismatic, rebellious, and I am shy, unconfident, adrift. They hold forth, spouting about philosophy, literature, theatre, art and politics, and I have nothing to add.

This academic path, studying English Literature and Language, French and History, is ready made for me and it is easy, and what Mum wants for me. But it seems unreal, and I can find no passion for study. Once I get into the swing of things, I am a half-hearted student, switching off the alarm and turning over to sleep in, missing the first couple of lectures for the day.

Someone steady

Robert's research is in quantum physics, something to do with measuring light energy from the stars; he is collecting data from equipment on the roof of the Physics building at uni, and processing the results on SILLIAC, the first computer ever built in an Australian university. In the process, he's discovered that he is more interested in programming computers than he is in collecting and measuring light rays; he wants a career in computer systems, but first, he has to finish his thesis. And whatever Robert starts, he finishes.

He tells me, when we start dating, that he became a teacher after graduating in science, because that was what his mother had done, and it seemed a good career for him. He taught in outback schools in Queensland for a few years; his unsatisfied yearning for higher knowledge inspired him to save up so he could enrol for a PhD at Sydney Uni. He supports himself by coaching maths in his spare time, and he always has money in his wallet. He's eight years older than me, more worldly than the boys I've been used to dating.

He takes me out for dinner to restaurants with a wine licence and a dance floor. These are the best times, for when he dances he is gay and youthful. I learn to respond to his rhythm; we jive like crazy and dance the slow numbers cheek to cheek, without words.

When my second-year university exams are over, we celebrate at an Austrian restaurant in the Cross. The wine is served in etched glass decanters; the glass globe is suspended in a wrought-iron frame shaped like a grapevine, and when you press your glass beneath it, the wine flows out. The wine is ordinary, but the serving vessel transforms it into nectar. It is a farewell dinner; he is going to Queensland to spend

Christmas with his family. Over coffee, he gives me a little parcel; it contains a pigskin cigarette case with Black Sobranie cigarettes. I've acquired a taste for these strong, cigar-like cigarettes with the gold-wrapped filters, but I can't afford to buy them myself. They make me feel older, more sophisticated.

I am touched by his elegant gift, and after we say goodnight and I lie in bed, I wonder whether I could come to love him. He seems reliable and attentive and I am tired of unrequited or unequal love affairs. It is nice to have someone steady, someone who isn't risky, who won't let me down.

My family was shattered by my father's betrayal of us, and I carry my mother's bitterness and grief as my shadow. She taught me that passion is dangerous and leads to despair and loss. That life is about security, loyalty and continuity, not change and adventure.

Mum likes Robert because he is ambitious and clever and can converse with her about politics and the state of the world. She likes the fact that he has a career path planned and is earning money, and that he seems more mature and sensible than many of my boyfriends have been. He doesn't have a distinguished background, but comes from middle-class Australian-Anglo-Saxon stock. Though his accent is very Aussie, flat and nasal, and he drives a pink car, a bit of polish will make all the difference, she reckons.

When he returns after Christmas, he dates me attentively, and soon we do it at his flat, making love his way. Lots of kissing and groping, and deep thrusts that end in him withdrawing and coming, while I lie back wondering if this is all. This smelly, clammy, warm pudding steamed from our mixed flesh. But there is the thrill of knowing I am doing something forbidden, secret, that my mother would be shocked, that I am a woman without her knowing about it. That makes up for the boring bits.

One night, we lie in the reflected light from the street, listening to the drone of traffic. His flat is on a smelly, noisy road where traffic hums past all night. I am half asleep when the phone rings. The clock says twelve-thirty a.m.

Robert gropes for the phone. 'Yes, Mrs. Anderson. Yes, she is… OK. We'll be there in half an hour.'

When we get home, Mum is sitting up in her dressing gown in the living room.

'Well, Robert, what have you got to say for yourself?'

'Er…I'm not sure what you mean, Mrs Anderson.'

'You know very well what I mean. I won't ask where you two have been. I want to know what your intentions are.'

Robert, for once, is nonplussed. He stands in the doorway, fidgeting in his pocket.

I move over to the lounge and watch the two of them lock wills.

'Well… I want to marry your daughter, of course.'

This is news to me.

He looks across at me. 'But…er…she's very young,' he fingers his moustache, 'and I'm supporting myself while I finish my PhD. I've got one more year to go. I…I think I'll be in a better position by about September. Then I'll just have the thesis to write up. But we'll have to live very carefully until I get a position in the department and Anna is able to support herself, at least till I make my way. I aim to be a professor by the time I'm forty. But the first few years will be…'

'Yes, of course. But Anna is on a scholarship and gets a small allowance. So I think you could manage. She's assured of a job at her old school when she graduates. In any case, I think the wedding should be this year.'

I know what she means. She isn't sure if we are having sex, but she doesn't trust us, and wants the safety net of marriage for me.

Robert nods and shakes her hand. He's lost for words, but the nod and handshake are his tacit agreement. He walks over and kisses me on the cheek. If this is a proposal, it is the best I will get.

When he is gone, Mum gives me a stern look and says, 'Go to bed now. And make sure in future you're home by midnight!'

Return to Arendal, 1996

The brighter richer emerald and forest greens of vines and vegetables in the Murrumbidgee Irrigation Area fade and mix with shades of grey, brown and black in the belt of trees that curves along the river's course. The land dries out and flattens into the monolithic architecture of the plains. My white rented Holden Commodore, more powerful than I'm accustomed to, masters the narrow strip of road that sweeps north of the river. In my childhood, this road was unsealed, a trap for inexperienced drivers caught in summer's red dirt corrugations that rattled and shook nuts and bolts, muscles and bones. In winter, the road's slippery surfaces lured vehicles into hopeless bogs of soft red mud.

My heart hastens as I near the entrance to the famous stud station, Ulonga, that was the earth to our moon. I drive in, hoping no one will see me, and I can sneak a look at a world I visited in my childhood. My only fragment of memory is of a tennis party at a rambling white homestead with red corrugated-iron roof, and a lovely semi-courtyard garden with lavender hedges encircling a bed of roses. The house is still here, but dilapidated, its only grace the weeping willows that surround it. No one is home except for a couple of dogs tied up at the back of the house. They greet me as if I am the first person they've seen for years. The tennis court and gardens are overgrown with weeds, and the approach road is full of potholes. My memories – a spacious, sprawling country house with cook and housekeeper, and a large family entertaining guests from a hundred miles around – don't fit this decaying, deserted place.

I drive away, up the red dirt track to the highway again. I scan the horizon for signs that the world I lived in is still here, hiding beneath years of change and neglect and the climate's fierce debridement of human effort.

A few minutes on, I reach the turn-off to Arendal. Perhaps, when I reach our place, the house will still be there, just as I remember it: tall sugar gums guarding house and garden; a simple cottage with arched roof, sloping to wide gauzed-in verandas front and back; a giant cedar, spreading its cool green umbrella over the roof; orchards on two sides, flower beds all round the house; vegetables swelling and flourishing in manured beds; and behind, the bend, the mysterious world where I played imaginary games, and paddled on sandy edges of the river that romanced our hard-working life. Perhaps my writing its story has brought that world back to life.

The approach road is on the opposite side of the fence now, making me wonder if I'm on the right track. It curves around, over a ramp where there used to be a gate. I pull up outside a house I don't recognise, in a spot where there used to be an open paddock and a chook yard.

I knock on the door of the house. A young woman comes out, a small boy clinging to her skirt.

'Hello. I'm Anna Anderson. I used to live here when I was a child, and I've come back to see the old place. Would you mind if I have a look around?'

'Sure. Help yourself.'

A brown kelpie dog slides round the corner, wagging its tail. I pat its smooth head and inhale its earthy smell, remembering our sheep dogs – kelpies, collies, kelpie crosses. They were my companions and our helpmates.

'Do you know when the old cottage was pulled down?

'Haven't a clue. My husband's the overseer here. This place belongs to Ulonga now.'

'Oh…well, I'll just wander round a bit.'

She nods and closes the screen door. The dog follows, tail waving graciously.

I walk over the ground where my father laid out and planted our garden, and built the sheds and outhouses. I find no trace of the world we shared, apart from the twelve sugar gums that still stand tall and proud, and a scraggy remnant of the cedar tree, that probably re-grew when the original was cut down. If you climbed up to one of the higher branches, you could see the horizon, and watch the ribbon of road that ran a mile north of our home paddock.

I find it hard to orient myself to where things once stood. Where were the shed, the wood heap, the laundry and the water tank? I catch my breath and laugh and cry when I discover some ruins of the old windmill, a few twisted blades in a pile of timber boards. Here it was that I tripped on the log and fell into the river. Here it was that Malcolm rescued me.

'Go and tell your mother and don't you dare cry,' Dad said.

For more than half my life those words have stuck in my mind. Was that when he died to me, the father I loved and trusted? Was it my father's ghost that left later carrying a suitcase? A ghost I didn't see again for forty years, when I decided to find him and hear his side of the story.

Gympie Hospital, 1988

He's lying on the hospital bed, surrounded by crumpled lumps of sheet, one leg bent, the other cut short above the knee. The stump is bound in swaths of bloodstained bandage. His face is grey and pain-creased. His eyes are empty windows in a derelict house. He doesn't hear me come in, so I step up to him and reach out my hand. My fingers touch his arm, feeling the slackness and sandpaper texture of his cold old skin. He turns and gazes at me.

'Dad? It's me, Anna.'

'Holly? It's you? My lovely girl. I thought I'd never see you again.' He grabs my sweaty hand with his heavy fingers.

His mind drifts between present and past. Sometimes, I'm little Holly, sometimes I'm forty-eight-year-old Anna. Sometimes he speaks of Mum as she was forty-odd years earlier, when she stood and watched our world fall apart.

Next day, I visit him again in the early afternoon. They've pushed his bed out onto the veranda. He's looking a bit more alive. His face is furnished. There's a hint of rose in his cheeks and a light in his eyes that weren't there yesterday. He talks for hours about Arendal. He tells me how he built it up and added to it, turning it from eighteen hundred acres to over eight thousand; how he built additions to the house and made the garden; how he built a shearing shed, a hut and an engine shed.

He asks me about Mum, about our life after he left. 'She was a wonderful woman. I always loved her the best. I wish it hadn't happened.'

I tell him she never looked at another man, and called him 'Daddy' till the day she died; how she told me she used to have orgasms with him when they made love. He is deaf, so our conversation is shouted. He dozes; a nurse wakes him to give him a drink.

'Holly…'

'Yes?'

'I made her happy for a while, didn't I? She had…what was that word you used?'

'Um…orgasms, Dad.'

'WHAT?'

'ORGASMS!'

'YES! ORGASMS! That was it!' He lies back with a satisfied smile.

The nurse giggles and looks at me quizzically. She's probably wondering why on earth I'm talking to a ninety-five-year-old amputee about sex.

I imagine what a charmer he was when he was young and handsome, and as a mature man. He took each situation in life as a challenge and a battle of wits. He's run out of bargaining power now. His physical body is a patchwork of parts. It's been cobbled together like an old motorcar that trundles on long after it should have given up the ghost. He left his first wife and family and the property he'd struggled so hard to create. He punished himself by enduring a loveless second marriage. Now he's crippled, poor and at the mercy of others. And yet he's still fighting, still challenging life.

As I sit by his bedside, I see how the nurses love him because of his feisty spirit and sardonic wit. One of them who comes to change his bandages teases him about being a wealthy man.

'Yes, well, I've only got one leg. What I'll do is find a bloke who's missing the other leg. Then we can share a pair of shoes and halve the cost, and I'll save money.'

After the nurse has gone, he sighs and grabs my hand. 'I'm not wanting to put your poor mother in a bad light with you, but you asked me in your letters to give you the facts. Your mother didn't play good cricket after I left. Perhaps it's not to be wondered at. It was a colossal job for a woman to do. I didn't tell her to get out when I came back, but I expressed disgust at the state the house was in and all around, and naturally it wouldn't have been possible to have us both there together, so I decided I would have to take it over again and knock it back into shape and clean it all up and sell it and divide the proceeds, and of course I came out the loser, what with the paying of the different accounts and fixing the windmill and the house, which was in danger of toppling over into the river. Other things missing were a big bay mare which was a beautiful horse, my good dogs, sulky and a lot else besides – wool and equipment she hadn't accounted for.

'I don't know how your mother explained to you children why I left but I was tried in a kangaroo court and condemned to Coventry without any evidence. And nobody ever made any attempt to hear the truth, and naturally your poor mother was not going to tell the awful facts.' He shifts his weight, and bends over with a groan; he lifts the pillow his stump is resting on, moving it closer to his other leg. He sighs again and closes his eyes.

I know the awful facts. I know that you lost heart and belief in the place, that you neglected it, that you escaped as much as you could towards the end, that you had an affair with the neighbour's cook, that you left Mum to bring us up and run the place on her own, that you took the income from it and paid her a paltry allowance, that you came back when she was alone and forced her to leave, that you sold the place and she had to fight you in court to get a one-third share of the sale price. That you never kept in touch with us, that you never tried to contact me or see what has become of me until I broke the silence forty years after you left. I don't want to know your facts, because they are not true. Whatever truth there was in them was lost long ago. You are trapped in the story you have made up. I feel sorry for you, but my childhood love is a ghost.

I sit by his bed for a few minutes, reflecting on what he has lost and what he destroyed. He's sleeping, so I leave him. There is no point in trying to tell him our side of the story.

Next day, when I say goodbye, he clasps his arms around my neck and cries. 'Holly, we both know we probably won't see each other again. I always loved her. But it all went bung. I wish it hadn't happened.'

I hold him for a moment or two, then disengage his arms and leave the room.

*

The truth that I know is the one that Mum and I shared in those hard, lonely years when he left. And the patterns set then, of abandonment and broken families, was the template for my adult life, but in mirror image. I left my first husband, and I lost my children. My life broke down in my thirties, after my children had been abducted by their father and taken to America to live. But that's another story.

When I ended up in hospital on bed rest for two weeks, I came full circle, back to those bitter times when it was just Mum and me, and I found that love was unreliable and could vanish like a mirage on the horizon.

The visit, Sydney Women's Hospital, 1974

'I think I made a mistake marrying Robert,' I say to Mum, who sits on the hard chair by my bed, wearing a lavender blue silk dress she made herself and a dark grey hat swathed in velvet ribbon. 'Once I married him, my life was mapped out for me, and I came to the point where I couldn't follow the path any more – I had to jump off, I couldn't keep going.'

'Hmm. Well, I kept going. When I suspected Henry was having an affair with Mrs Dalton, I couldn't make up my mind what to do – whether to leave him or stand my ground. I dreamed I was teaching in a big boys' school in Sydney. It had long corridors and lots of stairs. After I went to Sydney to see Vera off to England, I decided to stay on for a while. You remember, you stayed with Aunt Irene in Wollongong? I looked for a job. The one I took was at the school I saw in my dream. It wasn't a happy time. I found the boys very difficult to control, and often, when I was climbing the stairs to the classroom, I'd feel just as I did in the dream – exhausted and trapped.'

'Do you think you would've stayed there if you'd been happier with the job?' I ask, shifting my weight on the hard, crackly mattress.

'Perhaps. I can't say. I often rehearsed leaving Henry, and that was the only time I made an attempt at it, but something pulled me back to Arendal. I couldn't foresee what would happen – I just had a foolish hope we could start again.'

'Do you still love him?'

'What a silly question!'

She fusses with the catch of her handbag, opening and closing it.

'Well, at least you *did* love him, didn't you?'

'Of course I did! I adored him.'

'I thought I loved Robert, but I think now I just wanted security.'

'Security was something Henry and I never had. We had a dream of life on the land, but we didn't know what we were letting ourselves in for. It was my idea to get a place on the river. I dreamed it would be a little paradise. Anyone could've seen it wouldn't work, but no one advised us against it.' She sighs. Her fingers reach for a rose in the bunch of garden flowers she brought, and stroke the petals. 'When I met him, he was so ardent, full of life and fun.'

She opens her bag, takes out a cologne-scented hanky and blows her nose. 'I blame myself for the whole venture, really. My heart was set on it.' She stuffs the hanky back in the bag, pulls out her lipstick and renews the red outlines on her wide mouth, folding her lips in and compressing them to spread the colour.

I turn restlessly, wanting to ask her one more question. 'You know, Mum, Robert says I'm frigid. I never had orgasms with him.'

She looks at me, raising one eyebrow 'Oh. I see.' She is silent for a moment, looking down at her hands. Then she answers my silent question. 'I did have orgasms with your father. But I avoided having intercourse as much as possible, because I was afraid of getting pregnant again.'

'I guess I happened at one of those times you couldn't avoid,' I say, a smile tugging at the corner of my mouth.

'Well, darling, I was forty-five! But never mind, you were a gift. You were my last baby. You were plump with a floss of golden curls, and when you were big enough to play outside, you would sing and dance and talk to the plants and the insects and animals all day long. You were a joy and a blessing, and you were my lifeline in those years after he left. I couldn't have stayed on without you. And I know how hard it was for you.'

Tears sting my eyes, and I reach out and hold her hand tightly in mine. 'Thank you, Mum.'

We make a little more conversation, then Mum checks her watch.

'I'd better go, if I'm to catch the next ferry.' She pulls her gloves on and bends over to kiss my flushed face.

At least she hasn't changed her perfume, I smile to myself.

A visitation, Perth, 1982

Six months after Mum died, I was sitting in Perth in the hairdresser's, having a perm. It was a Saturday morning and the hairdresser had a woman helping her put the curlers in and apply the solution. The assistant was talking about how she was training to be a clairvoyant.

I felt sceptical. How can you train to be a clairvoyant? I thought. You either are or you're not, surely!

She turned to me and said, 'There's a woman around you. Is there someone you've lost recently in sad circumstances?'

'Yes,' I said, and burst into tears.

'There now,' said the hairdresser, with a cross look at her assistant. She handed me a tissue. 'It's all right. Yyou don't need to talk about it.'

'No, it's OK,' I said, looking at her assistant, 'I'm glad you said it. My mother died six months ago, and I wasn't there. I didn't know she was dying. She died alone.'

'Well, you know,' the assistant said as she patted a strip of cotton wool into place under the curlers, across my forehead and above my ears, 'our loved ones stay near the earthly plane for a while after they die, and when we think about them and mourn them, it draws them back and holds them near us. Eventually, we need to let go of them so they can move on.'

I felt guilty when she said this. The hairdresser set the timer and asked me if I wanted a magazine. I nodded, and she brought a pile and put them in front of me.

Celebrities. What do people see in all these stories of diets, addictions, affairs and jilted lovers, I wondered, as I leafed through *New Idea*. Stories of people's lives, all told to a formula. Real life is so much more complex.

I think of how, when I went to Sydney for the funeral, Vera told me that she'd been to see Mum in hospital one evening, and Mum had said, 'I'm so afraid that this is the end.'

'Of course it's not,' Vera said. 'You've been ill before and pulled through. We don't want you to die.'

Then she went home and went to bed with earplugs in. So she didn't hear the phone ringing in the early hours of the morning. And apparently they didn't ring David. So Mum died alone and afraid. I felt angry when she told me. And I was angry that David hadn't let me know how ill she was. He said, when I asked him, that they didn't realise she was dying.

I would have let her know I felt for how alone and afraid she was, facing her end, and I would have sat with her, stayed with her. We were together when our hearts broke, when my father left. I wish I'd been with her when she left this life.

The assistant walked over and stood behind me, meeting my eyes in the mirror. 'There's something else she wants me to say to you.'

'What is it?'

She smiled. 'She says not to feel guilty, that all is forgiven.'

Goodbye to Arendal, 1996

I stand at the edge of the bend. The kelpie trots off, losing interest. Even the river is changing, sludgy and degraded by pollutants, its natural weed bed destroyed by carp, sandy beaches gone, banks bare and muddy. The bend is much barer and harsher than I remember it. It looks as though fierce floods have swept through it, piling up dead branches and sweeping away contours. There is no soft winter grass as there used to be.

I walk down to a favourite swimming spot. It's widened out and lost its sandy beach and shady overhanging tree, which is now stranded below water level. The original meandering path of the river, narrowing and widening as the terrain allows, has been forced into a straighter, more logical course.

I pick up a handful of red dust and let the wind take it, scattering it over the dead leaves that carpet the floor of the bend. The wind gusts, the gum trees sigh and shake their boughs, releasing more leaves that flutter to the ground. For a moment, I feel Dad's presence. He died at ninety-seven-and-a-half, ten years' span of life more than Mum, who died in 1982. He wanted me to see the old place, to mourn for it, to let his spirit rest. As the dust trickled through my fingers, I say goodbye. Goodbye to him, whom I loved so much as a young child. Goodbye to the ghosts of my mother and father's marriage and the family they created, the dreams they shared. Goodbye to my self as a child. Goodbye to the place.

I turn back towards the car and drive off, chased by the dog as far as the ramp. Beyond the river, man-made canals and banks and crops in various stages of germination have been painted over the dun coloured canvas of the original landscape. Here and there huge silos stand out where once windmills and small clumps of trees stood. There are no rusty-red patches of soil any more. Nothing remains the same but the flat semicircular spread of the land, the line of trees that follows the winding course of the river, and the immense open sky.

This is a busy, productive landscape. Gone are the subsistence days of watching the weather and praying for rain. Rain still matters, but wool and meat are bad in the marketplace and crops are all the go. Irrigation seems to bring in a greater greed. Before there was need, but it was always at the mercy of lack and uncertainty. Now there is more certainty, greed rules and dictates the way the land is managed. Water means dollars, little more. There's a little recreational fishing perhaps, but there are few fish worth catching. The river is no longer the mystical natural force that binds the two halves of the circle together as it weaves its course through the plains. It is a commercial resource in which people invest so they can exploit it for as long as it lasts.

As I travel east, back towards the coast, the flat, canal-striped canvas of young green gives way to an undulating landscape, embroidered with rice fields, vegetable crops and orchards. I follow the road along the river for a while, reluctant to lose sight of the belt of trees that curves along the river's course.

Letter to Martha, 2017

When you said not to feel guilty, that all is forgiven, I think that what you meant was that you understand, not just why I left you and went to Perth, and why I couldn't be there when you died, but everything that happened. That you no longer feel betrayed and deserted, and that you see why, as an adult, I needed to do the things you found so hard to accept at the time. That you can see the cycles of abandonment and loss in your life and mine and my children's and that you are present still, at some level I cannot perceive or grasp, loving us, helping us to get through, to learn and to take something joyful and loving from what happens to us.

When I lost my children, you stood by me. I repeated Dad's pattern in that it was I who escaped from the territory of monogamy, but I never wanted to leave my children, and when Robert abducted them and took them to America to live I was determined to see them again and to love them to the end of time, no matter what. You understood this, though you couldn't understand why I had felt forced to leave my children's father. You gave me shelter, you were always there for me, and when he brought our daughters back to live in this country, even though I didn't have custody of them, you always loved them, spoiled them, made them feel welcome on holiday visits.

When I was in the darkest despair, you said, 'They will come back to you, Anna.'

'How do you know?' I cried.

'I just know,' you said.

And I believed you. And you were right, though they were separated from me for most of their childhood.

You loved me unconditionally and because you were such a rock in my life, I managed to stay alive during those years of separation from them, I never gave up hope, and I loved them as you loved me. It has taken me most of my life to realise it, but you have been my role model. Not of how to parent young children (I wasn't such a rule maker!), but of how to love your children unconditionally, how to stay true to them through everything.

You did a wonderful job in difficult circumstances. You brought us up, you fed us, you clothed us, you read to us, you loved us, you taught us how to read and write and think, how to respect ourselves and others, you believed in our gifts and our right to be well educated, and you put your heart into running the farm after Dad left. You did jobs you'd never been accustomed to or taught to do, you moved in a man's world and found ways of making do, selling a bit on the side when you could to provide little luxuries for your family and friends and yourself. You tried so hard to hold onto the dream you and Dad had begun together. You loved once, and I believe you never considered marrying again. You certainly never went out with a man.

For me, it was hard being your daughter, the youngest in the family. I was your baby, your other self, and I was your crutch after Dad left, and your wailing wall. You wanted me to grow up to be all the things you could have been in a different life and a different time. As I grew older and tantalised you with the promise of my intellectual gifts and disappointed you with my half-hearted attempts at an academic career and my disastrous exit from my first marriage, you judged me, but you never stopped loving me.

You said in your diary that your marriage to Dad had a fatal inevitability about it, 'though he had no prospects'. Robert had prospects aplenty; my attraction to him was the inverse, I think, of yours. You were attracted to Dad's charisma, his good looks, his confidence, his vitality and, I think, though you wouldn't have admitted it to yourself, to his sexuality. I was attracted to Robert's stability, his sense of purpose, his worldliness, his maturity.

But I, too, had a feeling of inevitability about marrying him. It was almost unheard of in 1960 in Sydney for a young girl to leave home and live with other young people. Girls either stayed home with their parents, or they got married. An adventurous few went overseas to see something of the world. Those who didn't go to uni got jobs, or did secretarial or nursing training. I wanted to escape from you, from the family net, and the only way I knew how to do it was to get married. So when the first eligible man appeared, I settled for him.

I knew at some level that it was not me he wanted to marry. It was who I seemed to be, a young middle-class girl who was sweet, intelligent and malleable, one who could be shaped into the wife and mother he had been brought up to choose. One who was the mirror image of the girl you had brought me up to be, only not so chaste, or at least, not with him. I had no experience of mutual love by which to measure our relationship. Even you and Dad, who'd married for love, and who, I believe, still loved each other when everything went wrong, were never loving with each other – not when I was around. Love was a mystery to me.

When I was little, I felt loved, especially by Dad, who hugged me and walked arm in arm with me in the garden, sang songs and told me funny stories and tales of his childhood. Gradually I learned there was another man, also my father, who was hot-tempered, unfair and unreliable. One day, when I was seven, they both left – the father I loved, the father I feared – carrying a suitcase, disappearing from my life. Over the next few years, the two fathers merged into one, living in a distant place, never writing to me.

I didn't know what I wanted in a man – how could I when I didn't know who I was? I only knew that I wanted to be safe, secure, not to be alone and make my own way in life, or live under my mother's thumb. Most of all, I wanted someone who would not abandon me.

You didn't abandon me, I see that now. Your love was like a rock, always there; uncompromising and enduring, with softer crevices where one could shelter and draw strength.

And you didn't want to let me go. When, after many years, I fell in love with a man from Perth, and after six months of indecision, went over to join him, you felt rejected, deserted, though you didn't show it directly. You were difficult, moody, critical, in those last few weeks before I left.

David told me that you'd been carrying on to him about me uprooting my life to go across the continent, chasing love, and he told you off. 'Bloody hell, Mum, give the girl a break!' I imagine him saying. 'She's been through so much, she deserves some happiness. She's not too old to have another child. She has a chance to start again. Let her go!'

I did have another child, my beautiful son, but the Perth man and I didn't manage a happy marriage. We had too much pain and loss in our separate pasts. And that's another story.

There's only one way to end this broken story, to close the circle.

The Last Song

This place you know

Your mind is an outback landscape, washed almost white in the glaring summer sun, with bare, flat plains and a faint line separating the land from the sky. The only vertical marks on this horizontal world are a line of fence posts, trailing off into the distance, a lone tree etched against the bleak sky, and, if you look behind, the straggly trees, dark grey-green-black, curling along the line of the life-giving river, mysterious in its depths and shallows, a presence you cannot see unless you approach it, but you can smell it, and when you are lying still at night, or resting in the afternoon, you can hear it, whispering its ancient song as it wanders through the land, knowing its way, carved out over thousands of years. This is not your country, but you dwell in it, and it is in your blood, your bones, your nerves, and it will never leave you, wherever you live, whatever you do, and when you die, it will always be this place, this place you know.

Epilogue

There's an easterly wind blowing across the plains. It smells of rain. The old woman shivers, and draws her shawl of saltbush green around her thin shoulders. She's finished covering this stretch of rusty-red, just in time. There'll be a big rain tonight, breaking the long drought. She twists her hook through some threads of the last ball, and drops it in her bag. She moves towards the river bend, taking shelter.

Acknowledgements

Names of people and some places have been changed to protect privacy. This memoir of my mother's and my experiences is drawn from archival records, my mother's handwritten memoir, and my imaginative reconstruction of her thoughts and actions and my own memories. It is my truth as I remember it and may not correspond to the memories of other living members of my family.

The memoir has been so long in gestation that to name all who have helped me to persist with it and shape it would fill several pages. So I will just name a few, and say that if your name is not here, it is in the spaces between the lines, among all the friends and witnesses who have cheered me along the way.

First and foremost, thank you, Julienne van Loon, for mentoring me as my creative supervisor for the first completed version of my story when I was studying for a Master of Creative Arts at Curtin University. You kept writing in pencil on my manuscript (we didn't work together online) 'Cut back'...'we don't need to know this'...'leave some space for the reader to imagine.' I learned the craft of writing from you, and I now pass these lessons on to my editing clients.

Barbara Milech, you were the first academic to whom I told my story, who encouraged me to write it, and who mentored me in postmodem and feminist theory and the craft of writing.

Thank you to the several friends and co-writers who have read versions of my story and have appreciated it and suggested changes: Maureen Helen, Elisabeth Hanscombe, Rachel Robertson, Marion May Campbell, Nicola-Jane le Breton, Marian Edmunds, Margaret Walker, among others.

Thank you to professional agents and publishers who have read and critiqued earlier drafts: Virginian Lloyd, Finch Publishing; Lou Johnson of The Author People; Aviva Tuffield of Black Inc.

Thank you to Alexandra Nahlous, literary editor, who did structural edits of *This Place You Know* in 2017 and helped me to shape it in its present dual form of my mother's story and mine interwoven with the theme of place.

Thank you to Mary Besemeres and Maureen Perkins, who were my supervisors for my PhD in Life Writing at Curtin University. Although not directly involved in my memoir writing, you have read much of my work and given me enormous support and encouragement to find my voice and tell my story.

Lastly, thank you, Ginninderra Press team, for your patient, thorough attention to detail in producing this text, and in creating a beautiful cover design.

www.ingramcontent.com/pod-product-compliance
Lightning Source LLC
Chambersburg PA
CBHW030905080526
44589CB00010B/147